BAUDELAIRE
A CRITICISM

BAUDELAIRE

A CRITICISM

By JOSEPH D. BENNETT

KENNIKAT PRESS
Port Washington, N. Y./London

The illustration used on the title page is
"The Outcasts," by Gustave Doré

BAUDELAIRE

Copyright, 1944, by Princeton University Press
Reissued in 1969 by Kennikat Press by arrangement
Library of Congress Catalog Card No: 78-85985
SBN 8046-0601-3

Manufactured by Taylor Publishing Company   Dallas, Texas

TO
R. P. BLACKMUR
AND
ALLEN TATE

—Hélas! Tout est
abîme,—action, désir, rêve, Parole!

PREFACE

I extend my thanks to R. P. Blackmur, Christian Gauss, John B. Rawls, and Ira O. Wade for their suggestions and criticisms during the composition of this work.

My aim in providing translations has been to transport accurately as great an amount of the suggestiveness of Baudelaire's language as I could, keeping at the same time to those English words closest to his. To this end, I have necessarily sacrificed rhyme and meter. It is hoped that the translations will aid the reader in grasping the original verses, which are printed with them. In the case of the prose excerpts, the translation is printed without a French text.

J. D. B.

CONTENTS

1

CHARLES BAUDELAIRE lived in spiritual and physical misery most of his life. As a child, he was passionately attached to his mother Caroline. The world of entrancing colors, smells, and sounds flowered for him around her person: her rustling crinolines, her silks, her jewels, her furs, her perfumes which intoxicated his hypertrophied sense of smell. Together they made trips to rare and silent houses which had mossy court-yards, Chinese drawing rooms, and secret chambers heaped with toys. Summers he spent in the country house at Neuilly where he watched the shifting patterns of color in the sun-sets, silent and peaceful:

> *Je n'ai pas oublié, voisine de la ville,*
> *Notre blanche maison, petite mais tranquille. . . .*

> *I have not forgotten our house close to the city,*
> *Our white house, small but tranquil. . . .*

But at the age of seven, the spoiled, fastidious, gifted Charles lost the undivided devotion and attention of his mother whose charm was in the harmony of her stately and subtle movements, rolling like a tall ship, imperceptibly:

> *Quand tu vas balayant l'air de ta jupe large*
> *Tu fais l'effet d'un beau vaisseau qui prend le large. . . .*

> *When you go sweeping the air with your full skirt*
> *You look like a fine ship which stands out to sea. . . .*

He lost her to a handsome, vigorous, and fortunate military man. And so Caroline came later to be *Madame la générale* and *Madame l'ambassadrice* Aupick. But imagine the effect of this new household, resonant with glory and military energy, upon the exquisite, tasteful child, who knew his whims were those of genius, and that his undisciplined diversions were slowly and profoundly informative. Aupick was noise and bustle, meaningless, ridiculous. And the Napoleonic military school at Lyons, drenched in continuous heavy fog, was Aupick all over again, for it emulated the Spartan system of training. The beautiful child poet, delicate, impulsive, and aristocratic to his fingertips, was awakened, François Porché tells us, by drumbeats and marched at half past five to wash himself in freezing water. Elegant and capricious, he was tormented by his schoolmates, for he strove to make himself as different as possible from them, the clumsy louts, the provincials, the Charles Bovarys.

He hated and insulted the kindly, honest Aupick. His mother, with her many official duties, was often separated from him, and when they were at home together, the General, the Ambassador, the Senator, stood between them. Like young Hamlet, he felt that his mother had betrayed him, for she had no right to belong to anyone else. And for Charles joy disappeared forever; hell began. Shipped off to the West African island of Réunion by the prudent General, who wished to interest him in a commercial career, he returned with his head swimming with exotic landscapes, negresses, and Creoles. He invented fantastic, shocking tales about his voyage "to Africa and Calcutta" during which he spitefully pretended he had been attacked by sailors. He loved to brood over pictures such as this: "My ancestors, idiots or maniacs, in solemn chambers, all of them victims of terrible passions." And when he received his inheritance, most of which he soon squandered and burdened with debt, he set himself up as a dandy and took to himself an ignorant and selfish mulatto concubine in whose felinity he immersed himself, loving to clothe her only in jewels, by the fireside.

But he grew poor, and she grew old, misshapen, and shrewish. Once he almost killed her, beating her with a candlestick until the pillow grew bloody. He was pressed for debts that compounded and increased every year, driving him from one cheap furnished hotel to another so that he never knew the peace of a home, of a hearth, of those cherished and beautiful possessions, such as books, pictures, statuary, carpets, vases, and draperies, in which the dandy delights. He was a fugitive and a diseased one, for he had contracted a venereal ailment. Hounded, depressed, and obsessed to an incredible degree by money-worries, he remained loyal to the cunning, vicious mulatto as long as he lived. He aided her after they ceased to share lodgings, a separation which caused him intense fleshly anguish. She helped him plan his faked suicide, by which he hoped to extort money from his tenderhearted mother. He took his opium in the form of laudanum, moderately as a gentleman should, and still dreaming, he requested his just place in the Legion of Honor and in the French Academy. He knew that his eighteenth century dignity and politeness, added to his literary genius, made him peculiarly worthy of such distinction. Rejected and stultified, he sulked and took his revenge in his diary, which he hoped some day to publish:

"If a man has merit, what could be the use of giving him a decoration? If he hasn't, he can be decorated, because that will give him a luster. To consent to be decorated is to recognize that the State or the prince has the right to judge you. Besides, if it is not pride, Christian humility forbids the cross [of the Legion of Honor].

"Glory is the result of the adaptation of a mind to the stupidity of the nation."

This is true, of course. But it was necessary for Baudelaire's pride to be bruised and frustrated before he could discover the futility and vanity of his selfish ambition. All of Baudelaire's final wisdom and humility comes to him by arduous experimentation, from humiliation, from excruciation. His renunciation at the end comes after long slavery not only to lust, but to pride and its exhausting miseries, miseries which may appear to be folly and petulance to the outside observer. It required the terrible vulgarity of the Belgians, who chewed on gold and breathed on it, to bring him to his knees. It was the last trial that he had to undergo before being admitted to the Grail of the Word. How he clung to Brussels, excruciating himself, refusing to leave that hell! "Then he went back into the fire which refines them." Surely it was a Purgatory, a penitential sacrifice which he devotedly made, knowing its completion would bring his liberation. He took his vows of humility, prayer, and industry, as we see from the last entries in his diary. Already resigned, release came quickly in the form of aphasia; his mind gradually expired; and his body shook itself to death some months later.

2

FOR FORTY-SIX YEARS this courtly gentleman lived, from
1821 to 1867. Until the last years, he lived like a Louis XV
who has been deprived of Versailles, deprived of the eighteenth century way of life, and forced to live in an era dominated by a vulgar, money-grubbing *bourgeoisie*. This Bour-
bon Louis took his pleasures not in the *Parc aux Cerfs* but
in a cheap furnished room with a mulattress. His *lever* was
elaborate; he took two hours to perform his immaculate
toilette every morning. But the only courtier was the maniac
on the bed, the raucous gesticulating Jeanne, rolling her
white nigger eyeballs, chattering incoherently like a mon-
key. His poverty and his creditors exaggerated his pride and
contemptuousness. He walked among all the depravity of
his *ménage* as if untouched by his own lust. His excellent
clothes, his immaculate cleanliness, his outmoded politeness, his carefully modulated voice, his precise and dignified
movements, the hauteur of his visage, and the sarcasm of
his remarks hid the stains of his vice, as the apparatus of
Versailles concealed the depravity of Louis the Well-Be-
loved. He was an alcoholic, but he never became drunk. He
took opium, but only in private, when unobserved. His
solitude was like that of the Sun King; too majestic, too
awful to be approached. One was transfixed by his arrogant
stare.

He called it dandyism, but it was much more than that.
It was a consciousness of his own uniqueness as a genius,
a child of the gods. It was not dandyism, but monarchism;
and he was the sole and absolute monarch: "The dandy
should aspire to be sublime, without interruption. He ought
to live and to sleep before a mirror." This mirror is his court,

{ 5 }

his palace, his Versailles: "Glory to Charles X," the last legitimate French king whose attempt to restore the *ancien régime* in all its pomp and arrogance brought in the rule of the *bourgeoisie* in 1830. Baudelaire was the Pretender who had been disinherited by the rabble; his loneliness was regal: "A sense of solitude since my childhood. In spite of the family and especially in the midst of comrades—sense of a destiny eternally solitary. Nevertheless, a very sharp liking for life and for pleasure." Like Vigny's Moses, his high calling prevented him from any genuine social intercourse. But he can give commands; he can voice his displeasure, his irritation, his boredom. Amidst his majestic detachment, he must, like Louis XV, be amused. He must have his pleasure. He can play the part of the mirror also. A cunning courtier, he flatters Saint-Beuve and Hugo shamelessly. His dandyism is in its roots Romantic, a longing for the golden age. He wants a chivalry, an aristocracy, a monarchy, a theocracy: "There exist only three respectable beings: the priest, the warrior, the poet. To know, to kill, and to create. All other men are taxable and workable at their lord's will and pleasure, made for the stable; that is to say, to exercise what are called the trades and professions." His contempt for the rabble, the *bourgeoisie*, and for democracy is that of a Louis XV. It is the epigrammatist's witty display, the contempt of the privileged noble who sees in all change an enemy of his security.

The dandy cannot submit to democracy; he must be recognized by privileges and honors; he must have his retainers to act as mirrors; he requires a court before which to be gorgeous, and to drop epigrams: "Dandyism is before all else the burning need to make oneself original, within the outside limits of propriety. It is a cult of the self. . . . It is the pleasure of astonishing and the proud satisfaction of never being astonished . . . a resolve never to be emotionally affected. Dandyism is the most rigorous of monastic rules. It is the last flash of heroism in the decadence. Dandyism is a setting sun; like the declining orb, it is superb, without heat and full of melancholy. But, alas! the mounting tide of democracy, which invades and levels all, drowns day after day these last representatives of human pride." The dandy is a Romantic projection of an ideal self which is pride incarnate. The dandy strives to be completely a se; uncaused, uncreated, independent of every social tie to family, friends, or nation. His only function is to exist; he is superb and his leisure is creative. "A dandy does nothing. Can you imagine a dandy speaking to the people, except to baffle them?"

Let us compare him with the man of affairs: "Some functionary or other, a government minister, a director of a theater or a newspaper, can be sometimes estimable beings, but they are persons without personality, beings without originality, born to perform functions, i.e., born to act as house servants for the public." When we know what Baudelaire thinks of the public—the rabble of democrats and bourgeois—the sneer in this passage is evident. We have seen it before in Byron's Don Juan, in Hugo's Hernani, in Goethe's Werther, in Châteaubriand's René, and in Musset's mal du siècle. Let us look at Baudelaire's Don Juan as he is rowed across the river of hell. The scene is like the Delacroix illustrations of Dante's Inferno:

Montrant leurs seins pendants et leurs robes ouvertes,
Des femmes se tordaient sous le noir firmament,
Et, comme un grand troupeau de victimes offertes,
Derrière lui traînaient un long mugissement. . . .
Mais le calme héros, courbé sur sa rapière,
Regardait le sillage et ne daignait rien voir.

Showing their hanging breasts and their open gowns,
Women writhed under the dark firmament,
And, like a large flock of offered victims,
Their long roaring dragged along behind him. . . .
But the calm hero, leaning on his rapier,
Looked at the wake of the boat and did not deign to
    notice anything.

{ 7 }

The dandy ignores the parents he has wronged and the women he has betrayed. He uses them as tools for his pleasure or his ambition; then casts them aside when they can no longer help him. No one has claims upon him, for obligations would be servitude for the dandy: "Forgetful of the past, content with the present and resigned to the future, intoxicated with his coolness [sang-froid] and with his dandyism, proud of not being as low as those who pass, he says to himself, contemplating the smoke of his cigar: 'What becomes of these consciences is of no importance to me.'" When the dandy is faced with an inevitable loss of independence, there is always suicide, the most rigorous canon of his monastic rule.

We may now inquire whether or not the dandy represents the Devil, since he is an incarnation of unlimited egotism and cruel pride. His elegance and his politeness are refined expressions of this hateful vanity. From this picture of the early dandyism of Baudelaire, we can appreciate the amount of travail and suffering which was required to purge him of it. The rest of his life is a story of slow agonizing *purgation*, by which the dandy, the pride-devil, was torn out of him, leaving alone within him the man of charity. Baudelaire, as dandy, was Pascal's man of intellect (*esprit*). But the man of the greatest intellect is infinitely far below the man of charity. According to Pascal's statement: "From all bodies and from all intellects, one would not know how to draw a movement of pure charity. It is impossible because charity is of another order; it is supernatural." Baudelaire is raised from the order of intellect to the order of charity by the slow infusion of this supernatural force upon him. He did not discover it; it was forced in upon him by his protracted humiliation and anguish.

The early dandyism is not completely diabolical; it is mixed with unusual wisdom. As Baudelaire develops, sainthood comes to be a part of the dandy ideal: "Before everything else, to be a *great man* and a saint for one's self." Yet

{ 8 }

the dandy thinks of his sainthood as a badge of his superiority over "minds like those of the Belgians, who can think only in partnership." At this stage, he sees no contradiction between being a *great man* and a saint. His sainthood is partly another means of manifesting his pride. His "self-purification" is often the obverse face of his "anti-humanity."

Dandyism provides him with the basis of attack against the utilitarianism of the modern era:

"Commerce is in essence satanic—Give me more than I give you.

"Commerce is *natural*, thus it is *infamous*. The least infamous of all the businessmen is the one who says: 'Let us be virtuous in order to make more money than the fools who are vicious.' For the businessman, honesty itself is a speculation in lucre. Commerce is satanic because it is one of the forms of egotism, and the lowest and vilest of all the forms."

We know that when Baudelaire says "to be a useful man has always appeared to me as something quite hideous," he means that the man "useful" for the production of material goods and services in a bourgeois or a socialist economy is useful merely as a machine is useful. Such a man has no spiritual life and no excesses. But Baudelaire at this stage will not pity this automaton; he must triumph over him and give vent to his *superbia* by implying "Thank God that I am not as other men" in his remark. His dandy's pride is involved with his wisdom. His dandyism is even the starting point for his brilliant analysis and denunciation of the doctrines of natural goodness, the danger of which he sensed. As he became more convinced of the natural evil in man and in his impulses, his dandyism came to be a barrier of artificial restraints—of courtesy, of religious restraints in the ethical sphere—which he set up against his natural impulse toward evil. But the danger of pride is still resident in dandyism when he infuses it with the ideal of sainthood, the life of religious restraint. He is constantly tempted to be proud of his momentary and infrequent successes in restraint, or of his mere advocacy, without enactment, of restraint. Then he uses his ideal of sainthood as an instrument of scorn, as in his attack on George Sand. Every word he says about her is true. But he cannot avoid making his unusual wisdom and insight a sort of triumph-festival, or field day for his own pride.

We can see this demon of pride ineradicably haunting his Journals and his criticism. The fact that he can scarcely suppress it gives us an idea of the intensity of his suffering. His pride was a much greater obstacle to him than his lust, or his use of alcohol and drugs. The dandy would of course consider himself able to suppress his lust and his use of stimulants. It would be part of his pride, his independence. A demon would certainly not be subject to these fleshy weaknesses; his diabolical pride would prevent them.

Baudelaire's suffering comes from tearing out his demon by the roots. If Baudelaire had been only a demon, he would not have suffered, nor would his flesh have been so weak as to cry out with pain when Black Jeanne was separated from him. The Journals give us the record of this suffering. We know that he suffered equally from himself and from "the tyranny of the human face." But when he had to confront both at once, he was sorely tried. When this exquisite man went abroad in the city, it seemed that he gave himself out, prostituted himself, exhausted his energy in facing every visage he saw. Crowds exhausted him; by the furious intoxication caused him through mingling with them, they drained him of all vigor. Each face was an obstacle that must be surrounded, dissolved, and assimilated by his consciousness, which, like an insatiable sphere, consumed everything within its ardent periphery. He could not provide the fuel for long; he cultivated his hysteria with delight and with terror. Now, he is always dizzy. And on the 23rd of January 1862, he feels the wind of the wing of imbecility pass over him. He has always had the sensation of the gulf—the abyss of action, of dream, of memory, of desire, of regret, of remorse, of the beautiful, of number—and now he has fear of sleep as one has fear of a great hole.

But there are, in this latter part of the Journals, notes about the dynamic morality of Jesus. He asks, "Is my phase of egotism finished?" Prayer is now his reservoir of strength, and humility has arrived. His humiliations have been the grace of God because they have led him to humility. "Blessed be God who gives suffering like a divine remedy for our impurities!" Only the man of charity is left: "Without charity, I am become as sounding brass or a tinkling cymbal."

In one of his last writings, a prayer which sums up the anguish of his life, he throws himself upon the infinite understanding and mercy of his Creator: "Lord, my God! you, the Creator, you, the Master; you who have made the Law and Liberty; you, the sovereign who allows all to be done; you, the judge who pardons; you who are full of motives and causes, and who have perhaps put in my mind the taste of horror to convert my heart like the cure, in the end, which a surgeon's knife brings; Lord, have pity, have pity on mad men and mad women! O creator! Can monsters exist only as monsters in the eyes of Him who alone knows why they exist, how they have made themselves such, and how they could have prevented themselves from becoming monsters?" Baudelaire prays here in spiritual stress: "Lord, my God!" He remembers and extols the Lord's law and judgeship even though he is condemned by this law. He is grateful for the terror which God has put into him, for it has brought him to fear his Lord. He knows he has been a monster of pride and lust; he feels the closeness of lunacy, "the wind from the wing of imbecility" at his ear. He blames himself for having made himself a monster. He does not blame God, but is utterly humble, opened out flat for his Creator to inspect, like a cloth on the ground. The process of Purgation is complete and he is ready to die.

3

AT THE END OF HIS PURGATORY, we found Baudelaire a religious man, ready for his Creator. But what sort of a religion? His religious feeling was all important to his life at the end. He was in the process of being saved; he had undergone severe religious experience in which he had been clawed open by Irresistible Grace. He certainly believes in the God of the Jews and the Christians. A sinner, he appeals to this God as both just Judge and dispenser of forgiveness. It is the same God that Descartes discovered at the end of his syllogism of universal doubt: the God about whom he had been taught, as a child, in the French Catholic schools. But did he believe in the divinity of Christ? Christ had been for some time "of Gods, the most incontestable." Yet, even by the time of his death, Baudelaire had not assumed belief in the Trinity. It is probable that at the time of his death, he was headed in that direction.

Baudelaire is close to the orthodox view of human nature. He stresses the natural depravity and original sinfulness of human nature. His religious consciousness develops from his knowledge of the evil within him and of the Devil attacking him through his corruption. He is thus orthodox on the most important point, the one which the nineteenth century refused to believe. But he is heretical in his constant emphasis on the absolute empire of evil and Satan over human nature. Grace never· comes to effect salvation. It would appear then that his tendency was toward Manicheanism: the Evil One is as powerful as God himself. Only at the end when he had been saved did he realize the omnipotence of the Christian God.

We must dismiss his youthful worship of Satan from any

serious discussion of his religious beliefs. He grew up in a literary atmosphere which considered Satan the hero of *Paradise Lost*. Satan was the rebellious Hernani defying his unjust ruler. He was a Byronic hero, wronged and defiant, the companion of Alpine scenery and thunderstorms.

The Satanism of his adolescence did serve to represent the attractiveness of vice throughout his life. It remained as a melodramatic background for his few unsuccessful poems—poems cluttered with the machinery of horror, rats, corpses, and demons. But Satan, though attractive, is never a sympathetic figure in the mature poems. He is, when successfully used, a terrifying symbol of the evil that is in every *hypocrite lecteur*. We must remember, too, that Baudelaire is not a theologian. As a poet, he has a right to exploit Satan as a symbol. It is a nice theological question how much of a Devil does exist; orthodoxy would say that Baudelaire's is too large, that he has assumed the proportions of the Manichean demiurge. It is, however, sound theology as well as sound poetry never to underestimate the power and cleverness of Satan—he is the constant companion of strength in the secular orders and is known even to the hieratic. The Devil is unfortunately much closer and much more present to most of us than the Paraclete. It is therefore allowable that he should appear in Baudelaire's work with strength undiminished by theological reservations.

The poet is concerned with arousing, juxtaposing, and fusing the paradoxes which inform our cogent experience. In doing so he orders it, or reconciles it. But he avoids systematization insofar as it is formal and deductive. He may feel (and generally does) that he has exceeded this level of discourse in that he has achieved suggestion and polysignification, that he has actualized rather than baldly stated the content of the situation which he exploits. He lays no claim to nor has he any desire to incur the laborious but necessary systematization of the responsible theologian.

The stylistic precursor of Baudelaire's Journals is Pascal,

which whets their surgical and dissective tactic; but more important, their ideological atmosphere is to a considerable extent Pascalian, and, insofar as it is, it supplies Baudelaire with standards for criticism which enabled him to exhaust the evils of his time as he concentrated his gaze upon the certain alternatives which the psychology, eschatology, and ethic of the tradition of Paul, Augustine, and Pascal afforded him. This background, with the aid of de Maistre and with the rejection of the ideas of the eighteenth century *philosophes*, gave him a power of criticism over his own age that was greater than Leconte de Lisle's or even Flaubert's.

Baudelaire used the Christian concept of human nature and destiny as a touchstone to expose the falsity of the ideas of the nineteenth century. Renan's *The Future of Science* is a good example of most of these nineteenth century ideas: overconfidence in human nature, in intelligence, in science, in progress, in the future. Renan opposed these ideas as often and as vigorously as he upheld them. But this work expresses the nineteenth century as much as Comte and Herbert Spencer did, with its mass of false predictions, shallowness of perception, and immaturity of mind, culminating in the painful: "We hold God quit of His paradise since celestial life is brought here below." To Baudelaire, "The century seemed to ask from black magic the means of raising itself suddenly to supernatural existence. This magic dupes them and lights a false happiness and a false knowledge for them." Because these ideas captivated his generation, Baudelaire was never appreciated. Viewed then as partially mad, he was possibly the sane man of his time. He stood almost alone; for Flaubert was not interested in sustained critical reflection nor did he share Baudelaire's approximated religious convictions.

Baudelaire attacked especially those ideas which cover up the contradictions and paradox in our experience by omitting those parts of it which give us difficulty. The doctrine of progress violates his experience of the depravity and destructiveness rooted in human nature which certainly cannot be removed by human craft or ingenuity. "As a new example and as new victims of inexorable moral laws, we will perish through that by which we have believed we can live." We have tried to live and progress by increasing our material comforts. We have abstracted physical well-being from the complex of man's necessities and have believed that he can get along and be happier with only that part of his personality being exercised. But the neglected part (which we have tried to atrophy) merely becomes warped and elongated into such hideous shape that we descend to the level of brutes while congratulating ourselves on our advanced state of civilization. "Mechanization will have so Americanized us, Progress will have so well atrophied our entire spiritual part that nothing among the sanguinary, sacrilegious or unnatural dreams of the modern utopians will be able to be compared to its positive results."

Matthew Arnold could not see this; he thought that poetry could control the positivist and scientific temper of the age, although religion had failed to do so. For Baudelaire, the devotion of the century to utility and commerce is evidence of its retrogression. It is a blatant and self-congratulatory display of egotism of the crudest sort. All functions except those of poet, priest, and warrior are given up to cupidity and utility. In politics, in secular life, "the brigands alone are convinced—of what? That it is necessary for them to succeed. Glory is the result of the adaptation of a mind to the national foolishness." Everywhere, society is rotted with universal, original sin and has no defense against it, for it does not recognize the existence of Satan.

In detecting his existence and in appraising his great power, Baudelaire has a defense against Satan; he has exposed him. Baudelaire is not duped by evil; he has branded evil as evil and in the act of naming, or identification, he has thrown up a protective buttress. We cannot say then that for Baudelaire Satan, having deposed God, is omnipotent. That would be true only for a man who does not believe in the existence of the Devil and who is thereby in bondage to him.

Baudelaire violently rejected the idea of man possessing *natural* goodness. Whatever charity man possesses comes as a result of spiritual effort and supernatural grace. As de Maistre had claimed, institutions and conventions are not responsible for evil; they exist to control the natural corruption of that "nature" in which the Enlightenment had placed its hopes. Baudelaire was among the first eloquent and persuasive secular writers to feel the enormous danger of the doctrines of nature and natural goodness. "Nature *teaches* nothing; she *forces* man to sleep, to drink, to eat. It is she alone who drives man to kill his fellow, or to eat him. . . . It is philosophy (I speak of the good philosophy) and religion which command us to nourish poor and infirm relatives. Nature (which is nothing else than the voice of our self-interest) commands us to beat them brutally. . . . Crime is natural. Virtue is *artificial*, supernatural, since it required gods and prophets to teach it to brutalized humanity, and since man *alone* had been unable to discover it. Evil is done without effort, *naturally*, through fatality; good is always the product of an art. All that I say about nature as a bad counsellor on the subject of morality can be conveyed into the realm of aesthetics." This exposure of modern Romantic ethical beliefs owes much to Baudelaire's dandyism. The dandy is created by artifice. He achieves his splendor by denying and suppressing his natural instincts. He lives a life of tension, as if on a stage, performing each act with delicacy and restraint. Dandyism, when its pride is expurgated, can lead the way to sainthood, that most heroic and difficult type of artifice.

Baudelaire's attack on the doctrines of natural goodness comes directly from his cardinal conviction and experience of the original, natural, universal sinfulness of man. It is this belief which informs all of his writings. Man is piteous, lamentable, surely damned; and all the more so because he feels he needs no help, that he can save himself by his own secular effort.

For Baudelaire then, the central problem is a religious problem. And the religious problem to him and to most men is most seriously apparent in the constant encroachment of evil upon them. Baudelaire has the clairvoyance which can see evil as evil in spite of *volupté*, and that "It is the devil who holds the strings which move us." His religious theme is the play of concupiscence and voluptuousness upon us; the terror and delight which our slow decline into hell brings us. Baudelaire's hell, like Dante's, is not for the other people; it is for us. The soul is sinking in quicksand and cries piteously for aid, and cries joyfully and gluttonously and boastfully for us to marvel at the revels and masquerades which crowd the deck of its silk-pennoned pleasure barge as the mud whirls up and sucks under its corners. This is the central paradox for Baudelaire, and, indeed for everyone, for it is the ethical problem, religiously conceived. Paradoxically, we relish our damnation, we seek it to avoid ennui, we find the climax of ecstasy in spiritual self-destruction. And our horror is increased by the certain knowledge which we have of this destruction in the very act of succumbing to exhilaration and stupefaction.

Behind the poems is persistent and meticulous scholarship which searches the problem of evil. Evil is not abstractly conceived in a proposition for metaphysical speculation. It is presented as it feeds on the marrow of men, as it incubates, and circulates within them. It tinges every thought and act, and instigates most of them, for morality, to the religious man, is mainly criticism, restraint upon previously incubated selfishness. Evil is irrational, inexplicable, impossible, and yet ingrained in every particular. In Baudelaire's poems, no corners are lopped off the problem to make it easy to get evil rationally explained.

In the ordered and climactic experience which these

poems arouse, the central paradox is still a paradox, unresolved. Stimulating and evocative, it works out in many concentric combinations which spread away from the poem and into our sensibilities as readers and bystanders, until we too are involved in the drama and participate in the evil thereof, like toy boats set rocking by the concentric, expanding ripples started in the water by the plunge of a rock. We correspond to the poem and to the paradox of evil much as the poet corresponds to the poem or snail-shell he leaves behind, and as the elements fusing within the crucible of the poem itself correspond to each other. The elements are selectively induced as representatives of experience. These elements are concentrated and compressed to fusion, like substances which will combine only at very high temperatures, but which, when once consolidated, form an indissoluble compound, a new integer which violates the independence of its components in forcing them to associate.

As a result, a whole has been formed vastly greater than the sum of its parts, and very different in significance and suggestion from what you would expect had a mere addition been made. In an addition, the resultant number would not have been an integer, a prime number, indivisible; but would have been subject to division and therefore merely the sum of all its parts, a whole which could be constructed and dismantled at will. Abstract poems, formed by addition, are not integers; they can be so dismantled, like exercises in problems of division in arithmetic, where the dividend has been previously designed to yield an even quotient when the proper divisors are applied.

Baudelaire's poems are concrete, which is another way of saying that they are paradoxical. Every concrete object is a mystery because, like a paradox, it cannot be solved or decided. It is in this respect that poetry renders our experience. It presents the paradoxes but does not explain them. It refines, channels, and sharpens for presentation the subtleties of the interplay and interdevelopment of these conjunctions of opposites. And it is the conjunction of opposites which lies at the basis of poetry, by its very form and technique, its rhythm, and especially by its central power and tool: the trope, or figure of speech. All figures of speech and metaphor depend on comparison. They harness two objects or facts in our physical or emotional cosmos which on the surface seem to have no relation. The labor of the figure of speech is to prove the relation that the poet believes to exist between the two terms he wishes to harness.

The conjunction of opposites (i.e., paradox) is the persistent and salient feature of our experience. This explains how the poem presents to us experience as valid as our own, even recapitulating, like the last entrance of the theme at the coda in sonata-form, the threads, the forms, the themes of our own past experience. And thus the relation of the poem to its poet and to its reader: it is the recapitulation of the principal themes.

THESE THEMES ARE PARADOXICAL and religious, or, more accurately, religious paradoxes. We are in the cosmos of Pascal, which is above all the cosmos of paradox; it is this excitation of paradox that dignifies Baudelaire as index, as integer, as symbol. When his poetry succeeds, it carries, resolved as if in climax, the complete burden—cyclical burden of strife and annulment, priestly burden of motion and rest, motion in rest. What it vivifies and represents is what is vivified in us when we lay claim to being alive, or when we appeal for exhumation from the wreckage and silt which cover the casual excursion and routine of our daily life. For our daily life is that part in us which shuns paradox, and to which paradox is abhorrent, and which pretends that paradox does not exist.

The Devil is part of paradox: as Baudelaire says, his most successful stratagem is to pretend that he does not exist. So long as we accept this stratagem, so long as we scrupulously (or desperately) adhere to the convention that he does not exist, we will have no means of defense against him—we are wholly within his power. We are then between his knees; his breath is upon us; his talon has marked us.

Paradoxically, God and the Devil exist in the same cosmos. Paradoxically the grotesque and the tragic are one; the "slightly deformed" is the beautiful; what is natural is abominable; what changes is both "vile and agreeable"; solitude and gay company are the same; cruelty and pleasure are the same, like extreme heat and extreme cold; love is seated in the place of excrement (as in the poem of Yeats); and free will and determinism are identical. Like Pascal, Baudelaire wants to account for all our experience; in accounting for it concretely, it is found to be paradoxical, contradictory. Consistency is not sought through abstraction; for abstractions are by definition incomplete and for the artist or the religious, less than true, unconcrete.[1] Therefore, the language of paradox must be used, for it alone is the adequate type of discourse for artist and religious.

The language of paradox is that not only of Pascal, Augustine, and Paul, but that of the Gospels, as in the Sermon on the Mount, and that of the Old Testament prophetic books. Paradox is abhorrent to the Greek mind, which feels it is a solemn duty to answer Zeno and Parmenides; and to schools of theology nourished on the Greek, such as the Alexandrians, the Scholastics, and neo-Thomists.

In the use of this language, religion and poetry form and order our experience by taking it up intact. The mysteries of God becoming man in the Incarnation; of man both sinner and made in God's image; of the omnipotence of God alongside the existence of Satan and evil; of man as a free agent capable of losing his soul and yet as guided and cared for by Providence; these are the central religious paradoxes. They are the final word about man's nature and destiny and they are all mysterious, the conjunction of opposites, the despair of the rationalist. But in their mystery and paradox they express the curve of our experience, and break in upon us irresistibly in our moments of sensitivity and tension. The religious life is one of constant stress, because in it the greatest reality is that of the joint existence of good and evil. Baudelaire participated in this religious life. But a life without paradox is irreligious. It is one in which either good or evil does not exist. It is the life of ennui, the most dreaded of states, because by it we lose

[1] In Baudelaire's sense, a poem is abstracted from a great number of experiences. But this selection is made carefully representative, so that experience is not ignored, but represented by a more illustrative exemplar of experience. The abstraction which I attack is that which ignores and sacrifices important elements of experience to gain consistency, rigorous simplicity, and strict deduction.

spiritual consciousness and become automatons, having knowledge neither of good nor of evil. There is no mystery, no paradox, no struggle.

Baudelaire is thus in opposition to both the major currents of his century: to Romanticism, which he survived, and to Comte's positivism which survived him into our own day. The latter movement bound the century to the set of abstractions which rules modern civilization. It borrowed the method of the pure sciences which had set up in their proper sphere the scientific laws, techniques, and laboratory methods which most efficiently exploit the natural realm. This realm is an abstraction—a realm of tabulated weights, densities, textures, and shapes. But the tabulated physical properties which indicate the usefulness of a particular rock for exploitation present only one of the many aspects of that rock which appear to our imagination and to our experience of the past.

Aesthetically and religiously, the rock is viewed in all of its aspects, concretely and even symbolically, as sign or metaphor; so that we see that the rock which science exploits is an abstraction, an hypostatized entity, whereas ours is genuine. The positivist, following Comte, uses the method borrowed from the true sciences to quantify not only nature, but man as well, into an abstraction as a set of processes, uses, drives, stimuli, and responses. His integrity is violated; the mystery in his experience is classed as delusion because it does not conform to the abstraction which the positive method sets up as the pattern and type of universal man, as the statutory touchstone and criterion to distinguish reality from dream and sanity from insanity. The positivist declares that the rock can be known only as an abstract collection of tabulated physical properties, and that man should likewise be known thus because he can be handled more efficiently when viewed as being such a collection.

Where Baudelaire calls paradox and mystery the irreducible integral truth about man's experience, the positivist excoriates this mystery as primitive superstition, dream, fantasy, subconscious drives, obscurantism. Baudelaire replies: "Civilized peoples, who still speak foolishly about savages and barbarians, soon you will *no longer be worth enough even to be idolaters.*"

Poetry to the positivist is not to give us knowledge about our experience, but to amuse and provide relaxation between the sustained periods of strenuous labor at abstraction and exploitation which make up what are believed to be our serious and important duties. The new era of control over nature through preoccupation with techniques and methods ushers in the world of ennui, the modern world of T. S. Eliot's wealthy woman: "What shall we ever do—the closed car at four, the hot water at ten?" The chase for exploitation, the quest for comfort, and the development of techniques are not of permanent interest. Whatever object is lusted for is speedily, efficiently, effortlessly achieved. The struggle between good and evil which actuated the cosmos of the religious has been *progressed* beyond; it can no longer provide interest or even diversion. Wormwood alone is left:

> Rien n'égale en longueur les boiteuses journées
> Quand sous les lourds flocons des neigeuses années
> L'ennui, fruit de la morne incuriosité,
> Prend les proportions de l'immortalité.

> Nothing equals in length the limping days
> When, under the heavy flakes of snowy years,
> Ennui, the fruit of sad incuriosity,
> Assumes the proportions of immortality.

Curiously enough, the positivist trend carried along with it the principal eighteenth century ideas of Romanticism which Baudelaire attacked. The belief in progress and in natural goodness continued, with its consequent rejection of the idea of sin. The Romantic movement influenced his poetry in addition, principally by his reaction from its formal and aesthetic practices.

The generation of Hugo, Musset, and Lamartine, immediately preceding Baudelaire, and the English generation of Wordsworth, Shelley, and Byron, upheld the theory of genius. The poet was a child of the gods; he spent lonely hours waiting for the wing of the Muse to touch him. When it did, he became the mouthpiece and instrument, the Oracle of the exhilarating pantheistic force which filled the Universe. The poet recollected in tranquillity the emotion transferred to him in his mystical union with Nature. When he felt he was inspired, he knew that every line he wrote was good and so he wrote as many as he could.

It is clear that the doctrine of natural goodness is behind the theory of genius and is responsible for it. Facility of style is encouraged by the feeling that an Oracle cannot make mistakes. Antithesis, shock, and contrast maintain the attention of the reader. The bizarre and the grotesque provide the inestimable shiver (*frisson*) which caused the enormous success of *Hernani*, *Ruy Blas*, and *Les Misérables*. The antitheses became regular, like anticipated cannon salutes, and the melodramatic reversals of situation became monotonous. But Hugo was fecund; he could turn out a new play, poem, or novel before the public became tired of its predecessor.

Hugo is the unparalleled orator and prophet of the generation. His habitual diction and poetic discourse is oratory. He apostrophizes in verse; he is grandiloquent, the Walt Whitman of his time. In his role of Oracle, Hugo harangues the rabble of the street crowds and converses with God on his tempest-tossed Channel island. God is not what you think He is if you got your ideas about Him in Sunday school. He is something much bigger, and better, a "more highly evolved concept." He is colossal, like a new and bigger airplane, skyscraper, or Hollywood extravaganza. He is the mystic pantheistic Force, lively, unlimited, unconscious;

{ 24 }

even Oceanic. And anyone should be able to converse with this unconscious force, which is of course at the same time the essence of consciousness. If you can't manage the conversation by yourself, you can enjoy it vicariously, by reading the poetic works of the intermediary and intercessory Oracle. Like Whitman, Hugo had his "religion which is bigger than the churches." "Let us join hands," Hugo writes to Baudelaire, and Baudelaire notes that this can only mean "let us join hands so that we can save the human race."

The poetic language of Hugo the prophet, and of Lamartine and Musset, the spoiled lovesick children, is stuffed with "vague, dizzying, and indeterminate" words which have value only for sound, filling in a line to give it the required number of metrical syllables. Profundity so-called becomes an excuse for shoddy workmanship. The didacticism of the prophet-Oracle in verse becomes likewise an excuse.

These were the dominant influences against which Baudelaire struggled and from which he reacted in his effort to compose poetry in the middle third of the century. Leconte de Lisle, making the same effort in this period, reacted so as to devote his poetry to metaphysical philosophical speculation, in spite of his great talent for brilliant descriptive metaphor and for sound. Gautier constructed his perfect medallions, his poems in cameo which aimed at exact description in emulating the plastic arts, especially bas-relief, to the exclusion of emotional elements.

5

WHAT DID BAUDELAIRE ACCOMPLISH within and beyond the barriers of his time? He accepted the doctrine of Gautier and Poe against moralization and didacticism. Poetry has only itself as an object. It should not be used for metaphysical speculation, for the development of ethical notions, or for any political or economic end. Thus Baudelaire opposes the philosophic poetry of Leconte de Lisle while admiring his small number of purely descriptive poems, such as the ones about animals. Nor does he follow Gautier's aesthetic. He takes objectivity as a discipline only and surcharges it with personal feeling—with anguish, with knowledge of sin, or with enjoyment of the harmony of *volupté*.

The discipline prevents the personal feeling in the poems from overflowing their objective frame into the subjective flood of Lamartine, Musset, and Hugo. Baudelaire does not wish to divert us with melancholy and joy, but to awaken us, to make us see clearly the mystery which surrounds our life. He brings us directly before the genuine problems by making them evident with unusual clarity. And clarity is out of place in the poems of his immediate predecessors. Vagueness of imagery and language chosen for sound give them a fuzzy effect. The images in such a poem may be interchanged; for the vague longing which they arouse and picturize is identical from image to image. The emotion aroused in such a poem is constant likewise. In this way the average poem, written in Baudelaire's period and before it, is a whole which is merely the sum of all its parts. Its words, images, and emotions can be interchanged at will, so that one image, word, or emotion represents all the rest, like columns in a peristyle. Thus the Musset, the Lamartine, the Shelley, the Swinburne poem is divisible by these constant elements as factors. It can be dismantled and reconstructed at will, for it all divides evenly. It contains no paradoxical elements which would make it a genuine integer. That is why it is so smoothly made and so pleasant and diverting to swallow.

It does not present the paradoxical aspect of sorrow or joy which makes irony their strongest vehicle. It gives us an undiluted emotion, drenches us in it without any relief. Many of us do not read the poem a second time. We know what it is about; it has no undertones and overtones of irony which can indicate the paradoxes that in their tension and interplay give a poem its eternal fascination. The fascination of the poems of Baudelaire is that they are surds; they cannot be dissolved; they are suggestive in that they actualize the genuine problems, but do not solve them. These problems and paradoxes are the ones outlined earlier in connection with the nature of evil and sin.

There is also paradox in the relation of the poet to the external world—paradox for which the keys are symbol, metaphor, trope—paradox in developing that external world to *correspond* with what we call an internal experience. The poet is then not only the maker, but the synthesizer; he who makes the forms to correspond; he who orders, reconciles, coheres our experience, preserving intact its paradoxical (that is, real, unresolved, integral, irreducible, inexplicable) nature. We might then define poetic knowledge as the ordering, the *correspondence*, of internal and external worlds for man.

"Permanent taste for prostitution in the heart of man, from whence comes his horror of solitude.—He wishes to be *two*. The man of genius wishes to be *one*, separate and inviolate and therefore solitary. *Glory is to remain inviolately one, and to prostitute one's self in a special way.*" The artist must paradoxically remain *one* and inviolate, must retain his individuality and at the same time participate in the personality of others, extending himself to the external world. He can do this only by drawing these other personalities and this external world into himself. As he draws them through his own focus, he reorients them and re-arranges them according to his angles of perspective. The artist can view all that is external to him as being a projection of his own personality, because it is a forest of symbols which correspond to his various states of mind or feeling. For him, nature is a dictionary, constantly suggestive and constantly reweaving its evocations in new and subtle patterns as the poet's sensibility plays over it. He integrates its suggestions into a projection of himself which is as changeable as his own states of mind.

The poet remains one because he has prostituted himself so thoroughly that he has assumed all his surroundings into himself and stamped them with the die of his vision, for they have been filtered through his own eccentric lens. His surroundings are raw materials which he prepares so that they will mix and correspond. The harmonies, reverberations, and correspondences between sounds, colors, and perfumes exist in Baudelaire's mind as it is projected into external nature. These harmonies are; therefore, all dependent upon the basic correspondence between the internal and external worlds of the poet and are valid insofar as the poet integrates the external world with himself, coloring it with his individuality.

In relation to the problems of composition and form, Baudelaire was a dandy. Rejecting the concept of genius-inspiration, he substituted artifice for natural overflow. His revisions are infinite, his labor is painstaking. His artifice is built up with a search for the exact word and the exact sound. Even when he uses "abyss" and "gulf," his language is clear and precise. He has a horror of vagueness and facility: "Except at the age of my first communion, that is to say at the age when all that treats of harlots and of silken ladders has the effect of a religion, I have never been able to suffer this de Musset, this chief of the 'swells,' with his impudence of a spoiled child who invokes heaven and hell for adventures worthy of the meal table of a boardinghouse, with his faults of grammar and of prosody, and finally with his total inability to understand the labor by which a reverie becomes an *objet d'art*. When one finally comes to be passionately fond of perfection alone, one disdains all these ignorant effusions."

When he speaks of perfection he is thinking, like Poe, of short poems, so arduously contrived that every line within the poem is a successful work of art in itself. In the perfect poem, as in Flaubert's perfect novel, all lines are equally good; it cannot be spotty, for no one part is better than another. But original spontaneity must remain the fundamental stuff out of which the poem is hewn. It is the essential rock which must be quarried before the statue is made. Baudelaire's success, like that of all great art, comes as a product of the tension between the spontaneity that gives birth to the organism and the discipline that shapes and prunes it. The discipline is the part which the artist adds to the unformed stuff; it is in this sense that the artist is said to create.

There are obstacles to Baudelaire's attainment of perfection aside from the universal poetic obstacle of the rock which must be hewn, and may possibly never be hewn correctly. One of these is his abuse of oratory and rhetoric. Another is his apparatus of horror imagery by which we often imagine he is merely trying to scare us.

In some of his verse, however, Baudelaire did approach his ideal. In this book, I shall take up a number of poems and sections of poems in which I believe he has done so. First, I shall investigate those poems which principally exploit the paradox of the existence of good and evil in man, treating the problem of sin. Next, I shall investigate those poems which principally deal with the despair and suffering of the victim, who is victim both of remorse for sin and of the misery of modern metropolitan civilization. In this section, the heart is symbol both of the peace of love that might have been possible and of the anguish that is actually present. Then I shall investigate those poems which present the pagan paradise of *volupté* as a refuge from pain and as a dream of peace, harmony, stately movement, and universal correspondence of shapes, smells, sounds, colors, and textures.

Baudelaire was the first important modern reaction against the early nineteenth century poetry. He worked his craft around the major paradox of good and evil. He revived an ironical form of treatment and a clarity of metaphor and imagery which had seldom been seen since the seventeenth century English poets. His actualization of paradox gave his work its incisive and disturbing power. His admiration for Gautier provided him with a technical discipline, a preference for tight and rigid verse form, which makes many of his poems seem like finely wrought crucibles within which a mass of molten metal is raging. This formal discipline coupled with his ability to actualize the paradoxes of experience gives his work an intensity that shames the work of his immediate predecessors and contemporaries. Gautier also gave him a model for objectivity—for keeping private difficulties and didactic comment out of his poetry. Instead of saying merely "I am desolate," or "I die, I faint, I fail," and thus begging his task, the poet must recreate for us through figures of speech, imagery, and suggestion his experience of desolation. A statement of feeling remains flat. But an actualization of the feeling draws us to life. It requires that we enter into the poem and undergo the experience ourselves by co-operating with the poem.

This requires spiritual effort. The reader must prostitute himself to the poem, but at the same time remain separate and inviolate. He brings the poem into his own cosmos and absorbs its order and knowledge into his own sensibility. We do not so much enter the cosmos of Baudelaire as we each arrange him into our own cosmos. And when we bring a successful poem into our own cosmos, we change the relations between all the baggage we are already carrying there. The addition of this newcomer inaugurates revealing adjustments. This is possibly what is meant by saying that a poem provides insight.

6

THE OPENING POEM of *Les Fleurs du Mal* broaches the central religious paradox: the question of the joint existence of good and evil; the problem of sin.

> *La sottise, l'erreur, le péché, la lésine,*
> *Occupent nos esprits et travaillent nos corps,*
> *Et nous alimentons nos aimables remords,*
> *Comme les mendiants nourrissent leur vermine.*

> Foolishness, error, stinginess and sin
> Labor our bodies and employ our minds,
> And we feed our pleasant remorse
> As beggars nourish their vermin.

"Au Lecteur" begins the treatment of the attractiveness of evil. Our spirits are occupied by evil; they are its demesne. It alone directs our bodies (*travaillent nos corps*) working them for its purposes, as a selfish foreman would work and abuse a gang of day laborers. Our sorrow for wrongdoing is ironically exposed. It is merely another pleasure: *nos aimables remords,* which we nourish to attract sympathy as, ironically again,

> *Nous rentrons gaiement dans le chemin bourbeux,*
> *Croyant par de vils pleurs laver toutes nos taches.*

> We return gaily to the filthy road,
> Believing we can wash away all our stains by con-
> temptible tears.

The most real and apparent force in our cosmos is Satan Trismegistus—thrice-powerful:

Et le riche métal de notre volonté
Est tout vaporisé par ce savant chimiste. . . .
C'est le diable qui tient les fils qui nous remuent.

The rich metal of our will
Is quite vaporized by this clever chemist. . . .
It is the devil who holds the strings which move us.

He rules us and we delight in his rule; we proceed to his hell *sans horreur.* But our subjection to him is underlaid by irony. We mock ourselves for being his puppets. And when we find the exact, the superb metaphor which expresses our pleasure at his rule, we find that it is a witty one:

Ainsi qu'un débauché pauvre qui baise et mange
Le sein martyrisé d'une antique catin,
Nous volons au passage un plaisir clandestin
Que nous pressons bien fort comme une vieille orange.

Like an impoverished debauchee who kisses and eats
The martyred breast of an antique whore
We steal in passing a clandestine pleasure
Which we press very strongly like an old orange.

Its irony gives it its strength, makes it the exact metaphor, because it introduces the paradox. Evil is not an unmixed delight. It violates our dignity; it makes us beasts. The superb mutually contributory metaphors of the harlot's breast and the orange make us see this; but in the subtlest way possible. We seem to discover this fact for ourselves, unaided by the poem. Seeking pleasure, we squeeze a shrunken breast as we would squeeze an old orange, clamping our strong teeth to it, draining it dry. We devour it without ceremony and without restraint, seeking immediate efficient satisfaction of our desire. But we are then paradoxically gaining pleasure from a disgusting, ugly object. We are beasts because we require no beauty for the satisfaction of our desire. We find pleasure in ugliness. Thus the suggestive and precise metaphor has given a vivid knowledge of the nature of evil which a thousand lines of didactic, moralistic poetry could never bring home. We have knowledge because we have contributed our effort to that of the poem. It has enabled us to find out the nature of evil for ourselves. This is characteristic of all of Baudelaire's successful imagery and poems.

> Et nous alimentons nos aimables remords,
> Comme les mendiants nourrissent leur vermine.

> And we feed our pleasant remorse
> As beggars nourish their vermin.

This simile likewise is ironical and likewise requires our effort in cooperation with the poem so that we may discover for ourselves the nature of remorse. It is a paradox that *aimable*—pleasant—remorse should be as vermin, for vermin are filthy and degrading to man; they suck his blood. In reading these lines we come suddenly to feel that remorse is pleasant, but that at the same time, paradoxically, it feeds upon us. And we think we have discovered this for ourselves, so subtle is the technique of the metaphor and so carefully restrained, almost hidden, to place the burden of discovery upon us. We have to scan meticulously the connection between remorse and vermin before we can discover the levels of irony concealed in their association.

> Sur l'oreiller du mal c'est Satan Trismégiste
> Qui berce longuement notre esprit enchanté,
> Et le riche métal de notre volonté
> Est tout vaporisé par ce savant chimiste.

> On the pillow of evil is Satan Trismegistus
> Who rocks our enchanted minds at length,
> And the rich metal of our will
> Is quite vaporized by this clever chemist.

The tone in this passage is one of voluptuous surrender to the enchantments of evil. We feel relieved of the labor of exercising our wills. But the irony is susurrant beneath the entrancing surface. The will is not only relaxed, it is *destroyed*, gradually, pleasantly, treacherously, like a tongue of metal immersed in acid. On the surface the metaphor is a smooth index of a pleasant trance. But its paradoxical irony—destruction through pleasure—works in on us after we have reread it, until we become conscious of the mine-galleries of meaning which lie beneath the surface level.

This image, together with the one of the *vieille orange* and the *mendiants nourrissent leur vermine* simile, are examples of Baudelaire's most successful use of figures of speech. All three of them—vermin, orange, and metal—have been sought in the realm of nature to provide precise correspondences to psychological states. In hitting upon the exact phrase, Baudelaire has harmonized or corresponded the external and internal worlds, the natural and spiritual realms. All are bound up together.

It is in this sense that the poet sees in nature *forêts de symboles* and calls nature *un dictionnaire*. There exists in nature a correspondence to every psychological state. It is the poet's job to find that correspondence—not merely to state his psychological state, as in "I die, I faint, I fail," but to find it in nature and actualize it in metaphor and symbol. Thus the poet tends to create his own exterior world and to project himself into it. He orders it and arranges it to express his sensibility. But it likewise orders and arranges him, as he draws it into himself. Again I quote: "He [man] wishes to be two. The man of genius wishes to be one, separate and inviolate and therefore solitary. Glory is to remain inviolately one, and to prostitute one's self in a special way."

"Au Lecteur" is unusually rich in successful metaphor. Baudelaire strikes the perfect phrase with amazing accuracy. He has described the process:

Je vais m'exercer seul à ma fantasque escrime,
Flairant dans tous les coins les hasards de la rime,
Trébuchant sur les mots comme sur les pavés,
Heurtant parfois des vers depuis longtemps rêvés.

I go exercising myself alone at my fantastic fencing,
Scenting in every corner the chances for a rhyme,
Stumbling on words as if on pavement blocks,
Bumping against lines long dreamed of.

Death rides in us every minute, slowly accreting in each sinful act like salt crystals dissolved in water which suddenly precipitate out when just that tiny crystal is added which saturates the solution and brings them, formerly invisible, out of the clear liquid to fall heavily to the bottom of the glass.

Et, quand nous respirons, la mort dans nos poumons
Descend, fleuve invisible, avec de sourdes plaintes.

And when we breathe, death into the lungs
Descends, invisible river, with smothered lamentations.

And from another poem, "Semper Eadem," when the heart has once given itself completely, death begins to draw it in for the harvest.

Quand notre cœur a fait une fois sa vendange,
Vivre est un mal! C'est un secret de tous connu,
Une douleur très simple et non mystérieuse,
Et, comme votre joie, éclatante pour tous.
Cessez donc de chercher, ô belle curieuse!
Et, bien que votre voix soit douce, taisez-vous!

Taisez-vous, ignorante! Ame toujours ravie!
Bouche au rire enfantin! Plus encor que la Vie,
La Mort nous tient souvent par des liens subtils.

When our heart has made its vintage once,
To live is an evil! It is a secret known to all,

A sorrow very simple and not mysterious,
And, like your joy, bursting forth for all.
Therefore cease trying to find out, O inquisitive,
And, although your voice is gentle, beautiful girl, be
   silent!

Be silent, thoughtless one! Spirit forever delighted!
Mouth with a childlike laugh! Still more than Life,
Death holds us often by subtle bonds.

The use of vendange—vintage—seems to me to indicate the ripening of the rich heart, and the taking-in of the vintage when the heart has given itself in all its mature ripeness, only to be trampled down into wine for the vats, fuel for the voluptuaries' fire. It is one of Baudelaire's most powerful metaphors. *Une douleur très simple et non mystérieuse, et comme votre joie, éclatante pour tous* extends the curve of the figure to a graceful conclusion—a restrained pain, yet strong and luminous—*éclatante*—explained as if to a child.

Death is mixed most intimately in those actions and sentiments which claim the whole being, the whole heart. It is woven with *des liens subtils* into our most expansive and profound joy, which becomes sorrow by its expansion. The shift in tone between *Taisez-vous, ignorante!, bouche au rire enfantin!* and *Plus éncore que la Vie, la Mort nous tient souvent par des liens subtils*, is the shift from banter with a child one loves, to a reverent and sorrowful illustration of one of the meanings of life to that same child. The banter and the lesson are alike in gravity; the banter is the suspense that is carefully caught up and shaded to drop us into the lesson without the least suggestion of shock. The shift in tone is incredibly smooth. The lesson fulfills the curve of rhetoric and rhythm initiated by the banter. The banter, infiltrating the lesson, welds the two parts so exactly that they seem to have melted into each other and yet to have remained distinct.

To return to "Au Lecteur," evil rides high in every human

breast, held back and increased in attractiveness by timidity and fear. The soul of the bourgeois Pharisee (whether a devotee of religious or commercial Pharisaism) is as rotten with vice and egotism as the murderer's:

> Si le viol, le poison, le poignard, l'incendie,
> N'ont pas encor brodé de leurs plaisants dessins
> Le canevas banal de nos piteux destins,
> C'est que notre âme, hélas! n'est pas assez hardie.

> If rape, poison, the dagger, and arson
> Have not yet embroidered with their pleasant designs
> The banal canvas of our pitiful destinies,
> It is because, alas, our spirit is not bold enough.

Le canevas banal! It strikes you immediately. We conceive our destinies pictorially. But they are banal, piteux. They are Watteau and Fragonard canvases—conventional reproductions of the "Eldorado banal." We long to give them the grandeur of sin—to achieve the damnation denied to shopkeepers and bank presidents. If we could attain genuine vice, we could find adventure and relish in life. Genuine vice is not excess, as most people understand it to be. It is the struggle that goes on in evil against good and that goes on within good to attain evil, just as virtue is the struggle in good against evil. We are all secret criminals: "All, in this world, sweats of crime: the newspaper, the wall, and the visage of man."

Baudelaire, in his famous apostrophe to the reader: Hypocrite lecteur,—mon semblable,—mon frère! (Hypocritical reader—my likeness—my brother!) is indicating that the attraction of evil is not peculiar to him, but is au lecteur—for the reader. He is also indicating his powers of absorption of the external world and self-projection: "Multitude, solitude: terms which are equal and convertible by the active and fecund poet. He who does not know how to people his solitude cannot know how to be alone in a busy crowd. The poet enters when he wishes into the character of everyone. The solitary and pensive walker derives a singular intoxication from this universal communion. He who easily espouses the crowd knows feverish enjoyments. This ineffable orgy, this holy prostitution of the soul which gives itself entirely to the unforeseen man who shows himself, to the unknown man who passes by."

The poet knows that the self-satisfied *lecteur* is *hypocrite*, because he has examined the race of *lecteurs, ses semblables*. He has observed that his own experience is true archetype of that of his fellows; he projects himself into his fellows and so orders their experience in his poem that it is index of the evil within them when they read it. Their experience is no longer a confused mass of temptations, consolations, and self-satisfaction as it was before they came to the poem. "Les Femmes Damnées," and the figures of Célimène and Harpagon in "L'Imprévu," are further illustrations of his power to enter alien personalities.

"Au Lecteur" concludes with the celebrated statement that ennui is the most evil vice and crime in which we can indulge. At first glance, this may seem to be the dandy's delight en *épatant le bourgeois*. Ennui, it would seem, certainly cannot be a crime, worse than murder or adultery. It appears on the surface merely to be innocent lassitude. For Tolstoy, boredom is the condition of *desiring* desire. For Baudelaire, ennui has the same meaning. Any desire is longed for, no matter how evil or destructive it may be. The bored man "would willingly make a debris of the earth" if it could amuse him. What restrains him from doing so is not religious discipline, but the disillusioning knowledge that he can derive no distraction from doing so; he can excite no desire in himself. Ennui is the punishment of concupiscence. The man who gives himself over to all desires is tormented by the failure of desire. Since desire has been the mainspring of his existence, providing it with its only interest, he has nothing to live with when it leaves except his rotted-out, abused soul. To be inescapably and eternally confronted with this horrible object is torture indeed. As Pascal observed, the most difficult thing for man is to sit alone with himself for any length of time, although it is only thus that he can be saved. He will clutch at any straw to divert himself. For Baudelaire, likewise, "all our unhappiness comes from having wished a change in place." Ennui, the desire for a change in place, is thus one of the principal circles in Baudelaire's Inferno. For Pascal, ennui can become an instrument of Purgation. It can purge the sinner by forcing him to contemplate his soul, his sin, and his destiny, thus concluding the period of ennui.

In addition to being the condition of *desiring* desire, ennui is also for Baudelaire a state of abstraction, of removal from the paradox which gives tension and significance to our life. Ennui removes us from the world of good and evil to an *abstract* world of moral and spiritual unconsciousness, where we are not troubled by the asymmetry of the principal paradoxical problems of life. Ennui convinces us that the Devil does not exist; that he is a childish or a medieval superstition, fantastic and impossible. So rid of the Devil, the person possessed by ennui does evil, not knowing that it is evil. He is then firmly in the Devil's grasp, having fallen victim to his strongest ruse. He who does evil knowing that it is evil and that the Devil is drawing him on to it has a defense and a dignity. He may exercise his corroded will at any time and call a halt. He may break off in the midst of a string of murders. The victim of ennui cannot call a halt; he will continue to murder, or defraud, or commit usury automatically, because he supposes that it is not evil. He is an automaton, a puppet, without will.

> Je suis comme le roi d'un pays pluvieux,
> Riche mais impuissant, jeune et pourtant très-vieux . . .
> Rien ne peut l'égayer . . .
> Ni son peuple mourant en face du balcon. . . .

Le savant qui lui fait de l'or n'a jamais pu
De son être extirper l'élément corrompu,
Et dans ces bains de sang qui des romains nous vien-
nent, . . .
Il n'a su réchauffer ce cadavre hébété
Où coule au lieu de sang l'eau verte du Léthé

I am like the king of a rainy country,
Rich but impotent, young and nevertheless very old . . .
Nothing can enliven him . . .
Not even his people dying in front of the balcony. . . .
The wise man who makes gold for him has never been
able
To extirpate from his being the corrupted element
And, in those baths of blood which come to us from
the Romans, . . .
He has not known how to warm up again this stupefied
corpse
In which the green water of Lethe runs in place of
blood.

Satan lives in the victim of ennui; he attacks the conscious
sinner. The consciousness of sin can release from ennui.
The consciousness that the evil in our lives is overcoming
the good makes life dramatic and gives significance to every
moment of it, just as the reverse process in the saintly Christian makes every moment significant in view of ultimate
redemption.

Baudelaire's Satan is not a Byronic hero, although that
idea is present in his youthful poems, where God is presented as "the tyrant gorged by the sobs of tortured mar-
tyrs," where Cain "mounts to the sky and throws God upon
the earth," and where Satan is Bacchus, god of pleasure.
The idea of Satan represents the fact that as free agents
we have the power to transgress divine law. The concept of
Satan is the necessary concomitant of the concept of free

will. Paradoxically, we cannot be free without also being subject to evil. The religious life is the purification and perfection of freedom, so that it may, with Divine grace, be proof against evil. The religious life is laid in the cosmos of Pascal; it is tension, strife, paradox. Though he is relieved from the subtler pangs of ennui, the sinner is tormented by the realization of his abandonment to evil all along the route of degradation. This torment is *l'immortel péché*, *immortal* sin because our capacity for sinning in abuse of our freedom raises us above the beasts or the victims of ennui, Dante's Trimmers, who have no consciousness of sin. "Pleasure wears us. Work strengthens us. It is necessary to work, if not through liking, at least through despair, since it is well verified that working brings less ennui than amusing oneself."

"Au Lecteur" introduced us to Baudelaire's Inferno, which is for us; not for the other fellow or the conventional villain, such as the capitalist or the labor leader. It entails a belief in both the divine and sinful potentialities of the fallen human spirit. It is a belief in the validity and all-importance of spiritual phenomena which are ignored in the modern world of abstractions, ennui, control-techniques, and therapy: "The abolishers of souls [materialists] are necessarily the abolishers of *hell*; they are, to be sure, acting in self-interest. At the very least, they are people who are afraid of rebirth; they are lazy."

There is a connection between this passage and the play upon rebirth, death-in-life, and life-in-death in T. S. Eliot's *Waste Land*. To awake from the cosmos of ennui and abstraction to a consciousness of good and evil, and the mystery that surrounds our experience, requires a strenuous gestatory effort, a spiritual rebirth. Complacency has fear of it, for it means death to one kind of life. Baudelaire's consciousness of the necessity of a belief in sin to make life meaningful was perhaps aroused by Joseph de Maistre, Catholic theologian and political philosopher for whom "original sin explains all, and without which one explains nothing."

"A Celle Qui Est Trop Gaie" gives us a specific example of the power of evil working through the sinner. As he wrote to Flaubert: "I have perceived that, all the time, I have been obsessed by the impossibility of accounting for certain actions or sudden thoughts of man without the hypothesis of the intervention of a wicked force exterior to him."

The poem displays this force working itself out in sadism, brutality, bitterness, and revengeful spleen which, when exposed in the violent act or wish, give a warm rush of physical ecstasy.

> Quelquefois dans un beau jardin
> Où je traînais mon atonie,
> J'ai senti, comme une ironie,
> Le soleil déchirer mon sein;
>
> Et le printemps et la verdure
> Ont tant humilié mon cœur
> Que j'ai puni sur une fleur
> L'insolence de la nature.
>
> Sometimes in a fine garden
> Where I was dragging my colorlessness,
> I have felt, like an irony,
> The sun tearing open my breast;
>
> And the spring and the verdure
> Humiliated my heart so much
> That I punished a flower
> For the insolence of nature.

It is the rancor and fever of the blood, excited by a malevolent external force which arouses this inconsumable restlessness: "Cruelty and voluptuousness, identical sensations, like extreme heat and extreme cold." The sun breaks in upon his *atonie*, his colorless state of mind. The sun lashes across him and scalds him with the knowledge of the freshness and simple tranquillity which he could have possessed, had he exerted his will against his concupiscence. He is driven wild by the *humiliation* of realizing the futility of his attempts to secure happiness in following evil. He exacts from himself and inflicts upon himself the most violent sensation which he has in his drab repertoire: sadism.

The use of *soleil* and *fleur* is superb symbolism. They project into nature the exact timbre of his misery. The sun hits him as it does a drunken man who awakens at noon after a night of debauchery. The sun is *comme une ironie*—like an irony; it recalls to the sinner how pitiful his egotistic search for pleasure and pride is in comparison with the peace and knowledge of usefulness in the divine order which the laboring sun suggests, symbolizing the daytime world of work and purposive activity, in contrast to the moonless night of concupiscence. The use of *une fleur* symbolizes the freshness and innocence which might have been his, but which can now give him relief only as a victim to his furious brutality. The use of these two images—*le soleil* and *une fleur*—in drawing on the external world to suggest an emotional state is that of which Baudelaire spoke in "L'Art Philosophique": "Pure art is to create a suggestive magic containing both the object and the subject, the world exterior to the artist and the artist himself."

In connection with Baudelaire's use of brutality as a temporary respite from states of extreme tension, we may bring forward these lines from "L'Héautontimorouménos":

> *Je te frapperai sans colère*
> *Et sans haine, comme un boucher, . . .*
> *Et dans mon cœur qu'ils soûleront*
> *Tes chers sanglots retentiront*
> *Comme un tambour qui bat la charge.*

I will strike you without anger
And without hate, like a butcher, . . .
And in my heart, which they will make drunk,
Your dear sobs will resound
Like a drum which stirs the attack.

Here, as in "A Celle Qui Est Trop Gaie," the same excruciating restlessness and spasmodic wrenching of the marrow
and the nerve filaments is brought on by the consciousness
of the inadequacy of the sensual pleasures to satisfy one's
boundless thirst for satiation. Again this tension is for a
time relaxed in a sadistic act, as if a human sacrifice were
required to appease the reigning inner demon of concupiscence.

Baudelaire's power of entering into other personalities—
"The poet enters when he wishes into the character of
everyone"—revives in "L'Imprévu" two complacent and
self-righteous sinners—thoroughly modern and typical characters from Molière. For them, of course, the Devil does
not exist. The characters appear in separate stanzas, disconnected in reference to each other, except that they are both
examples of that complacency which does not believe in the
Devil and which thereby acknowledges his rule.

Harpagon is Molière's *L'Avare*. Célimène is the super-
cilious society widow enamored of the artificial drawing
room life and gossip of her time, and beloved by *Le Misan-
thrope*.

Harpagon, qui veillait son père agonisant,
Se dit, rêveur, devant ces lèvres déjà blanches:
"Nous avons au grenier un nombre suffisant,
Ce me semble, de vieilles planches?"

Célimène roucoule et dit: "Mon cœur est bon,
Et naturellement, Dieu m'a faite très belle."
—Son cœur! Cœur racorni, fumé comme un jambon,
Recuit à la flamme éternelle!

Harpagon, who kept watch upon his dying father,
Said to himself, dreamily, before these lips already white:
"We have in the garret a sufficient number,
    It seems to me, of old planks?"

Célimène coos and says: "My heart is good,
And, naturally, God has made me very beautiful."
—Her heart! Shriveled heart, smoked like a ham,
    Recooked in eternal flame.

Three more disconnected stanzas follow, moving from a
gas jet, to a voluptuary, to a clock, all of which speak in
turn. It is a masterful exhibition of wit and irony, the most
successful in poetry since the seventeenth century English
poets. It is almost out of the mouth of Laforgue, in its sudden and ironical shifts of tone. This passage of Laforgue's
might have appeared in "L'Imprévu":

Celle qui doit me mettre au courant de la femme!
Nous lui dirons d'abord, de mon air le moins froid:
"La somme des angles d'un triangle, chère âme,
    Est égale à deux droits."

That which ought to show me how to manage women!
We will say to her first, in my least chilling manner:
"The sum of the angles of a triangle, dear heart,
    Is equal to two right angles."

We may compare Célimène's heart, the heart of Voltaire,
rational, astute, and reserved, to that of Baudelaire, cited
earlier in "Semper Eadem":

Quand notre cœur a fait une fois sa vendange,
Vivre est un mal! C'est un secret de tous connu,
Une douleur très simple et non mystérieuse.
Et, comme votre joie, éclatante pour tous.

When our heart has made its vintage once,
To live is an evil! It is a secret known to all,
A sorrow very simple and not mysterious,
And, like your joy, bursting forth for all.

Douleur for Célimène would be to give an unsuccessful soirée. Her heart is *naturellement bon.* We have a text from Baudelaire's letters which remarks on this kind of virtue. "What is the naturally good man? The man naturally good would be a monster, I mean a God. . . . [The idea is] pure *quixotism.*" She believed she was naturally good in the same way George Sand did. She need make no spiritual effort; she need merely follow her instinct toward the good.

Baudelaire is thinking of George Sand when he describes Célimène. George Sand had "advanced" ideas on every subject:

"She has always been a moralist. She is stupid, she is heavy, she is a chatterer. She has, in moral ideas, the same depth of judgment and the same delicacy of sentiment as the concierges and the kept women. She claims that true Christians do not believe in hell.

"La Sand is for the *Dieu des bonnes gens* [the God of the good folks, nice people], the God of the concierges and light-fingered servants.

"One should not believe that the Devil tempts only men of genius. He doubtless despises imbeciles, but he does not disdain their assistance. Quite to the contrary, he founds his great hopes on them.

"Look at George Sand. She is above all, and more than anything else, a *stupid animal* [*grosse bête*]; but she is *possessed.* It is the Devil who has persuaded her to trust to *son bon cœur* [her good heart] and *son bon sens,* so that she would persuade all the other stupid animals to trust to their *bon cœur* and their *bon sens.*

"I cannot think of this stupid creature without a certain trembling of horror. If I met her, I could not prevent myself from throwing a holy-water vessel at her head."

For Baudelaire, Célimène—and she includes a great many since the eighteenth century—is damned. Harpagon and Célimène are persistent modern types of those who caused Baudelaire to exclaim: "I am bored in France, especially because everyone there resembles Voltaire." The imagery describing Célimène's heart is Baudelaire at his most powerful:

> —Son cœur! Cœur racorni, fumé comme un jambon,
>   Recuit à la flamme éternelle!

> —Her heart! Shriveled heart, smoked like a ham,
>   Recooked in eternal flame!

Shriveled and hardened—racorni—by covetously looking out for its own interests. Toughened by wariness, sharp practice, and rational contempt for weakness, superstition—any mystery—until it is as dehydrated, wiry, and sinewy as a hardened, but reddish, smoked ham, hanging and swinging on its cord from the breastbone, as if from the roof of a smokehouse. It is the heart of Voltaire. It is even more tough and lumpy because it has been cooked in eternal flame, like a roasted nut.

We are amused by Célimène's petty arrogance while she is unknowingly damned. But the irony enriches and lays the foundation for our recognition of the tragedy of her situation. The irony opens us up to a realization that her situation is actual, that it may happen to us. It is not merely "something we read once in some poem." Thus it gives the most compelling moral wisdom, without being didactic: "A genuine work of art has no need for the speech of the public prosecutor. The logic of the work suffices for all the postulations of morals, and it is for the reader to draw the conclusions from the conclusion."

The logic of the poem is expressed through irony which enables us to discover the moral conclusion ourselves. We learn by making a co-operative effort with the poem. Irony, a special form of paradox, lays us open to the continuity between our own experience and the subject of the poem, because irony brings intact before our eyes the contradictory nature of significant experience: "The mixture of the gro-

tesque and the tragic is agreeable to the mind, like dis-
cordances to blasé ears."

"L'Examen de Minuit" is the best example of Baudelaire's sincere religious feeling. It presents the disgust and
shame of the sinner who recognizes what he has abused
and violated.

Nous avons blasphémé Jésus,
Des Dieux le plus incontestable!
Comme un parasite à la table
De quelque monstrueux Crésus,
Nous avons, pour plaire à la brute, . . .
Insulté ce que nous aimons
Et flatté ce qui nous rebute.
. . . Salué l'énorme Bêtise,
La Bêtise au front de taureau;
Baisé la stupide Matière
Avec grande dévotion,
Et de la putréfaction
Béni la blafarde lumière.

Enfin nous avons, pour noyer
Le vertige dans le délire, . . .
Bu sans soif et mangé sans faim!
—Vite soufflons la lampe, afin
De nous cacher dans les ténèbres!

We have blasphemed Jesus,
The most incontestable of Gods!
Like a parasite at the table
Of some monstrous Croesus,
We have, to please the brute, . . .
Insulted what we love
And fawned upon what we find repulsive.
. . . We have bowed down to enormous stupidity,
Stupidity with a bull's forehead;
Kissed stupid matter

With great devotion,
And blessed the pale light
Of putrefaction.

Finally, to drown
Dizziness in delirium, . . .
We have drunk without thirst and eaten without hunger!
—Quick, let us blow out the lamp, in order
To hide ourselves in the darkness!

The use of Croesus as symbol displays the attraction to us
of all the sterile pleasures—*Fleurs du Mal*—which throb in
us from some brutish energy deep within the sensual appetites. If uncontrolled, this power of evil, possessed like
Croesus of every worldly delight, makes us hang on the
rich and vulgar king, clutching for his stupefying food, which
binds us closer and closer in his power. Croesus, the Devil,
loaded with gold, seeks to pervert men into beasts—*bêtise*
in the shape of a bull—of violent purposeless stupidity. The
blind craving and itch of the lowest forms of animal life
for unescapable ecstatic pangs and for putrefied nutriment
is the pit dancing before every sinner. Pascal knew it: it is
"the Abyss." It is implicit in all of the poems and the title
of one, "Le Gouffre":

Pascal avait son gouffre, avec lui se mouvant . . .
J'ai peur du sommeil comme on a peur d'un grand
    trou, . . .
Et mon esprit . . .
Jalouse du néant l'insensibilité.

Pascal had his abyss, moving with him . . .
I fear sleep as one fears a great hole, . . .
And my mind . . .
Craves the insensibility of nothingness.

The hunger and thirst of our concupiscence are like flame;
they are sterile; they deteriorate us. But unfortunately we
cannot be consumed and find relief in extinction.

Enfin nous avons, pour noyer
Le vertige dans le délire, . . .
Bu sans soif et mangé sans faim!

Finally, to drown
Dizziness in delirium, . . .
We have drunk without thirst and eaten without hunger!

We drink without thirst and eat without hunger. Our desires do not satisfy bodily functions, but rage inconsumably. The delirium that we wish to arouse is like that induced by drinking salt sea water. Drinking sea water gives us the *pleasure* of feeding our thirst but does not supply water for the bodily functions. Instead, it increases our thirst with every swallow until the bitter liquor drives us mad with desire. There is no savor for us in the pleasures of concupiscence if the Devil possesses us so thoroughly that he determines us irresistibly as his puppets to dance for him.

This is the gulf, the crater which smokes on the horizon of the religious life: "Jerusalem—for if it is there that death has been trampled underfoot, it is there also that death has opened its most sinister crater." Christ has saved us; but the fact that He did appear makes it possible for us to deny Him. Since we know He exists and redeems, we are damned if we turn away from Him and degrade ourselves. This is the suffering and the happiness of the Christian. This is the paradox of the religious life, the tension and opposition which keeps the spirit a continuous agitated spark. A furious angel swoops down from the sky like an eagle, seizes the miscreant by the hair and says, shaking him:

"You know the rule! Know that you must love, without grimacing, the poor, the wicked, the crooked, the stupefied so that you can make for Jesus, when He passes, a triumphal carpet with your charity."

But "Le Rebelle," the damned man, keeps answering, "I don't wish to." This cosmos of struggle between good and evil is to the cosmos of ennui and abstraction as life is to death or stupefaction.

"Femmes Damnées" is the best example of Baudelaire's presentation of a situation which is developed as an illumination of the moral problem, but deftly, imperceptibly, without didacticism. Baudelaire, in his essay on Hugo, has described his own method: "It is not a question here of that preacher's morality, which by its manner of pedantry, by its didactic tone, can spoil the finest pieces of poetry, but of an inspired morality which slips, invisible, into the poetic matter like the imponderable fluids into the whole machine of the world. Morals do not enter this art as its object; they mix with it and blend with it as in life itself."

The Lesbian women, Delphine and Hippolyte, are symbols expressing in their deed and their spiritual distress Baudelaire's conception of the sterility of lust. Their particular lust, as most sterile of all, is but the type of all lust. Lust rages and wrenches the spirit which can never be consumed by its fires and thus can never find surcease. The caresses of normal heterosexual lust:

> . . . creuseront leurs ornières,
> Comme des chariots ou des socs déchirants;
>
> Ils passeront sur toi comme un lourd attelage
> De chevaux et de bœufs aux sabots sans pitié. . . .

> . . . will hollow out their ruts,
> Like chariots or lacerating ploughshares;
>
> They will pass over you like a heavy, harnessed team
> Of horses and of oxen with pitiless hooves. . . .

The use of ornières and chariots suggests constant, brutal wear and deterioration. Together with attelage of draft animals, the impression of casual, transient use of the body is set up. Partnership in lust is like that between an equipage and the road it travels. It must use the road to get to its destination, but it cares not at all about the condition of the road once it has gotten past. Therefore, the horse and chariot willfully deteriorates the road, if it can thus gain speed, not caring whether the next equipage can use it or not. All this seems to me to be contained in Baudelaire's use of the image of horse and chariot, *lourd attelage*, and ruts, *ornières*, to symbolize the relationship of partnership in lust. The body is left exhausted, a devastated battlefield where the soil has been so ravaged that no new life can grow. For lust, being purposeless and destructive, does not bring new life out of its warmth. It burns its creative force in arsonous flame until only the shell of the gutted body is left; but the inconsumable soul burns on.

Lust, whether heterosexual or homosexual, breeds upon itself and swells its thirst until it possesses completely, day and night, like a demon which has usurped the spirit. It is no longer a pleasure, but an agony which is determined upon its victim; she cannot resist it because the demon which possesses her causes the fibers of her physical and sensual being to demand this torture:

. . . *Je sens s'élargir dans mon être*
Un abîme béant; cet abîme est mon cœur.

Brûlant comme un volcan, profond comme le vide;
Rien ne rassasiera ce monstre gémissant
Et ne rafraîchira la soif de l'Euménide
Qui, la torche à la main, le brûle jusqu'au sang.

. . . *I feel enlarging in my being*
A gaping abyss; this abyss is my heart.

Burning like a volcano, profound as the void;
Nothing will satiate this groaning monster
And nothing will refresh the thirst of the Eumenide
[Fury],
Who, torch in hand, burns it even to the blood.

And again, the girl says:

> Ma Delphine, je souffre et je suis inquiète,
> Comme après un nocturne et terrible repas.

> My Delphine, I suffer and I am restless,
> As after a nocturnal and terrible meal.

Lust, like a cancer, seizes the heart and closes off its habitual charity and sympathy. The heart's energies are now focused on raw appetite, and appetite assumes the entire being so that it is but a single wave of desire. The blood changes into an acrid smoking liquor which sears the veins. Cannibal masochists, the women have made their meal upon themselves, providing their own tissues as fuel for the pyrotechnic exhibition which amuses them. The most monstrous pleasure of lust brings an aftersensation which is conventionally termed "shame," but which is presented more concretely here, as close as language can come to the actual sensation itself, by the use of metaphor. Baudelaire leaves us with this superb metaphor: *Nocturne et terrible repas;* he does not moralize. Indeed nothing more could be said. The metaphor brings the state of mind as close to us as is possible. It is violent and shocking. Didactic comment can only appear abstract and lifeless beside the symbolical representation, which is concrete.

Similarly, the juxtaposition of the Fury *l'Euménide,* her torch, and the burn as close as the blood, brings to bear the concrete weight of the Greek myth in all its connotation of sleepless, unallayed fever of the bone, blood-guilt, blood-lust, and blood-penalty. "To give one's self up to Satan, what is that? It is to abandon one's self to 'the joy of descending.'" The descent is toward brutality, the life of the lower animals. But man cannot live on that level, except with acute remorse and spiritual anguish. The fallen angel struggles inside of the brute:

Un ange, imprudent voyageur
Qu'a tenté l'amour du difforme,
Au fond d'un cauchemar énorme
Se débattant comme un nageur,

Et luttant, angoisses funèbres!
Contre un gigantesque remous
Qui va chantant comme les fous
Et pirouettant dans les ténèbres, . . .

Où veillent des monstres visqueux
Dont les larges yeux de phosphore. . . .

An Angel, imprudent traveler
Whom love of the deformed has tempted,
To the depths of an enormous nightmare
Struggling like a swimmer,

And fighting in mournful anguish
Against a gigantic whirlpool
Which rushes along singing like a madman
And pirouetting in the shadows,

Where viscous monsters with large
Phosphorescent eyes are watching

This is the irremediable hell because the fallen angel's consciousness is never extinguished. He cannot "sleep the sleep of the brute" (*Dors ton sommeil de brute*). He is "jealous of the insensibility of nothingness." The whirlpool—*remous*—is a powerful symbol of the gravity-pull downward of the centripetal gulf, the pit, the abyss. It is in constant motion, never leaving its victims to rest in peace. It is insane, it sings shrilly and dances with abandon. Like the wind of Dante's circle of the carnal sinners, it reminds the damned sinner of his purposeless, incessant activity and lust during his life on earth. The whirlpool of Baudelaire's Inferno demands struggle but never permits release through drowning. The phosphorescent monsters are the brutes, the lower forms of life, which are accustomed to this habitat. They have no souls to be lost or from which to suffer eternally. Untouched by the wing of the angel, they sleep the brutish sleep, and look on, without consciousness.

Baudelaire possibly chose Lesbian rather than heterosexual lust for "Femmes Damnées" because he wished to illustrate that deformity and perversity—unnatural qualities—are part of vice and crime; that the sinful is what revolts against the harmony and order which is the basis for the moral life— moral life which is at the same time the truly aesthetic life. Morality and aesthetics are nearly the same: "What exasperates the man of taste in the spectacle of vice is its deformity, its disproportion. Vice injures the just and the true, revolts the intellect and the conscience; but as an outrage to harmony, as dissonance, it wounds more particularly certain poetic minds. I do not believe it is scandalizing to consider every infraction on morality, on moral beauty, as a type of fault against universal rhythm and prosody." The moral influence of a poem is indirect and thereby more powerful. It suggests rather than dictates moral wisdom. The reader seems to discover the moral for himself. He enters actively into the labor of discerning what is the moral act. "I believe simply that every *well made* poem and *objet d'art* suggests a moral naturally and forcibly. It is the business of the reader to draw it in. I have even a very decided hatred against exclusive moral *intention* in a poem."

I feel that the apostrophe close to the end of Part I is a serious defect to the poem. It introduces without excuse the entire corpus of conventional horror-imagery which runs through all but his finest poems. It is thoroughly tasteless after one has gone through the *Fleurs du Mal* the first time. The apostrophe is presented with extreme rhetorical accentuation. Bombastic, exaggerated, it might have come from Victor Hugo:

> —Descendez, descendez, lamentables victimes,
> Descendez le chemin de l'enfer éternel.

and so on. *Lamentables victimes—le chemin de l'enfer
éternel—plongez au plus profond du gouffre où tous les
crimes—bouillonnent pêle-mêle avec un bruit d'orage—des
miasmes fièvreux—parfums affreux*—we have met all these
images so many times that they hardly seem meaningful
to us; we habitually skim over them to get to more significant matter.

On this estimate of the apostrophe I am in disagreement
with Mr. Kenneth Burke, who finds that in this apostrophe
"the stylistic efficacy of this transition contains a richness
which transcends all moral (or unmoral) sophistication:
the efficacy of appropriateness, of exactly the natural curve
in treatment."[1] I would agree with Mr. Burke that an apostrophe would have very great effect at this point in the
poem, but I feel that we have been given the wrong one,
a bungled one or, more certainly, a lazy one. I think that
Baudelaire's standard horror-machinery is used to cover his
laziness. When he is tired of a poem, when he can only get
one or two stanzas of a poem, or when he needs an ending
for a poem, he drags it in and then lets the formula do the
work for him.

In the midst of the apostrophe, we are aware that we have
arrived in that portion of the Inferno of Dante where Paolo
and Francesca and all those who sinned through lust are

---

[1] Kenneth Burke, "Psychology and Form" from *Counter-State-
ment.* Mr. Burke was the only critic I found who dealt seriously with
the technical and textual aspects of Baudelaire's poetry, and this in
one paragraph on the "Femmes Damnées." The remainder of Mr.
Burke's paragraph is of interest: "Here is morality even for the god-
less, since it is a morality of art, being justified, if for no other reason,
by its paralleling of that staleness, that disquieting loss of purpose,
which must have followed the procedure of the two characters, the
femmes damnées themselves, a remorse which, perhaps only physical
in its origin, nevertheless becomes psychic."

blown about by violent winds, signifying the purposeless fury of their passion:

"The storm of hell, which never rests, leads the spirits with its rapine; whirling and smiting it molests them.

"I learned that to such torment the carnal sinners are damned who subject reason to lust."[2]

As in the case of Paolo and Francesca, the nature of the punishment derives from the quality of the pleasure itself.

Ombres folles, courez au but de vos désirs;
Jamais vous ne pourrez assouvir votre rage,
Et votre châtiment naîtra de vos plaisirs.

Mad shadows, run to the object of your desires;
You will never be able to satiate your rage,
And your punishment will be born from your pleasures.

For the *femmes damnées* plunge in a gulf

. . . où tous les crimes,
Flagellés par un vent qui ne vient pas du ciel,
Bouillonnent pêle-mêle avec un bruit d'orage.

. . . where all crimes,
Lashed by a wind which does not come from heaven,
Boil pell-mell with a noise like a storm.

These lines just quoted, by placing the *femmes* definitely in Inferno, prepare for the finest stanza of the poem:

L'âpre stérilité de votre jouissance
Altère votre soif et roidit votre peau,
Et le vent furibond de la concupiscence
Fair claquer votre chair ainsi qu'un vieux drapeau.

The harsh sterility of your pleasure
Makes your thirst more thirsty and stiffens your skin,
And the furious wind of concupiscence
Snaps your flesh like an old flag.

[2] Inferno, Canto V: 30-34; 37-40. Inferno XV and XVI and Purgatorio XXVI, which specifically present sinners guilty of unnatural lust, do not describe their sin but deal with their significance as political, historical, or literary figures.

Baudelaire has given up depending, in this apostrophe, on rhetoric and stock imagery. He has brought to life before us in one image both the quality of the suffering of *femmes damnées* and of the fit punishment for their type of sin. The wind of lust cracks them out, whips open their folds as if they were old flags. And these flags are made of skin toughened, wrinkled, wizened, and made leathery by prolonged abuse in the wind. The flag's complete submission to the capricious, cruel, and absolutely determining wind is the exact simile. The additional overlay of similarity between the violent snapping, incessant curling and uncurling of the flag in a stiff wind and the convulsions of a body possessed by the despotic and sadistic demon of lust makes this image the most brilliant I can find in Baudelaire. Their lust, unleashed and magnified, becomes their punishment.

In Part I, a specific scene involving two women has been developed so that it can be transferred to Inferno. In Part II, we no longer observe a special situation, but view the entire circle where the carnal sinners have been placed in hell. The poet groups them carefully for us:

> *Comme un bétail pensif sur le sable couchées,*
> *Elles tournent leurs yeux vers l'horizon des mers, . . .*
> *D'autres, comme des sœurs, marchent lentes et graves*
> *A travers les rochers pleins d'apparitions. . . .*

> Like a pensive flock of cattle lying on the sand,
> They turn their eyes towards the horizon of the seas, . . .
> Others, like sisters, slow and grave, walk
> Through the rocks which are full of apparitions. . . .

The comparison with Canto V of Dante's *Inferno* is of some value. In Baudelaire's poém, Part I shows us a scene in modern life, above ground, and then works into Part II, where a scene in a generalized hell under the ground is presented. The power in Baudelaire's poem lies in Part I, where he develops the psychology of the sinner during and after her fall, summing up in the magnificent *vieux drapeau* image. The scene in hell itself is more of a sketch, a tentative fantasy. It is an imaginative picture, a plastic creation. There is no tension, no climax.

In the *Inferno*, Canto V is arranged as a unit to bring about the final climax when Francesca tells of the seduction scene during her life above ground. This scene is tied inextricably with the scene in hell below. The story of their former happiness is related during their present punishment; it succeeds from our interest in the lovers themselves who have been carefully brought forward from the background of the Second Circle, Circle of the carnal sinners—at first under the metaphor of starlings and cranes being buffeted in the cyclone of Inferno. Upper and lower realms, earth and Inferno, are conjoined in the present misery of the lovers and in the story of their former life in the world. This fusion brings the tragic climax. Everywhere, the hand of poetic genius of the first rank disciplines and orders, bringing together with perfect control the elements of his dramatic situation.

Baudelaire's poem, "Femmes Damnées," is by comparison sprawling and diffused. The material is not worked to a climax; the *femmes damnées* talk each other out before Baudelaire brings in the apostrophe; and then disappear when Inferno, with a new cast of characters, is reached in Part II. We see no ordering and unifying structural genius. The poem is allowed to ramble leisurely, working one vein till it is played out and then moving to another. It is relaxed; Canto V of *Inferno* is tense, straightened, channeled, and diked so that when its sluice is opened, extreme and orderly impact is the result. Baudelaire's poem has, however, struck valuable ore in Part I. The situation he chose and his initial manner of exploitation are excellent. But there is too much. He cannot leave the women's conversation until it is completely exhausted, and then the poem runs in all directions, destroying itself. This is his attempt at the long poem, a genre which, after Poe, he felt was inferior, and he obviously cannot handle it. Dante would have concentrated the Delphine-Hippolyte situation and rendered it in a few strokes, moving on then to build it into an underground hell. Baudelaire is a Dante only "in fragments," which it is for ourselves, as readers, to put together.

"Femmes Damnées" develops the theme of lust until its close connection with death is apparent:

Je veux m'anéantir dans ta gorge profonde,
Et trouver sur ton sein la fraîcheur des tombeaux!

I wish to annul my being in your profound throat,
And find on your breast the freshness of the tomb!

The pleasures of lust are like those of the tomb. They disintegrate us. They drop us into that gulf of stupefaction and forgetfulness which provides the attraction of the tomb. The murderous nature of lust is still more apparent in the use of torture to arouse pleasure. Sadism is inextricable from lust and indicative of its deathly nature. The last important image of the poem presents this:

Qui, recélant un fouet sous leurs longs vêtements,
Mêlent, dans le bois sombre et les nuits solitaires,
L'écume du plaisir aux larmes des tourments.

Who, hiding a whip under their long garments,
Mix, in the somber wood and the solitary nights,
The foam of pleasure with the tears of torments.

The pangs of lust and the agonies of death are the same. Both contain no real happiness; both are forced in upon us, determined, from the outside. The nature of lust is to kill and maim, as in "A Celle Qui Est Trop Gaie" and "L'Héautonti," to work off its craving for consumption and destruction and thus expend its accumulated and harrowing nervous energy. But in the expense, the craving is only rendered more intolerable:

J'ai cherché dans l'amour un sommeil oublieux;
Mais l'amour n'est pour moi qu'un matelas d'aiguilles.

I sought forgetful slumber in love;
But love is for me only a mattress of needles.

The blood-craze of lust attempts to bring its victim to physical and spiritual *death*. In all its seizures and impulsions it is striving to this final goal. "Love resembles strongly a torture or a surgical operation. . . . Do you hear these sighs, preludes to a tragedy of dishonor, these moans, these cries, these death rattles? . . . And what could you find worse in the question applied by careful torturers? These revulsed eyes of a sleepwalker, these limbs whose muscles burst forth and stiffen as if under the action of a galvanic pile [electric battery]—intoxication, opium, delirium will certainly not give you such frightful, such curious examples. And the human face, which Ovid believed to be fashioned to reflect the stars, speaks no longer except with an expression of mad ferocity, or *relaxes itself in a sort of death*. For surely, I would commit a sacrilege in applying the word 'ecstasy' to this kind of decomposition."

This relationship between lust and death is a fundamental rapport in Baudelaire's poetry. It is a central metaphor out of which much of his auxiliary imagery develops:

La Débauche et la Mort sont deux aimables filles,
Prodigues de baisers et riches de santé,
Dont le flanc toujours vierge et drapé de guenilles
Sous l'éternel labeur n'a jamais enfanté. . . .

Et la bière et l'alcôve en blasphèmes fécondes
Nous offrent tour à tour, comme deux bonnes sœurs,
De terribles plaisirs et d'affreuses douceurs.

Debauchery and Death are two friendly sluts,
Prodigal with kisses and rich with health,
Whose loins, ever-virginal and draped with rags,
Under eternal labor have never brought forth a child. . . .

> Both the bier and the recessed bed fecund in blasphemies
> Offer us in turn, like two good sisters,
> Terrible pleasures and frightful charms.

Both lust and death are sterile, bringing forward no new life, *toujours vierge* although *sous l'éternel labeur*. Throughout the poems lust is approached only with horror. It is described generally in terms of a metaphor either of torture or death:

> L'amoureux pantelant incliné sur sa belle
> A l'air d'un moribond caressant son tombeau.

> The panting lover inclined over his beautiful one
> Seems like a dying man caressing his tomb.

And again:

> Je m'avance à l'attaque et je grimpe aux assauts
> Comme après un cadavre un chœur de vermisseaux.

> I advance to the attack and I climb to the assault
> As a choir of little worms goes after a cadaver.

The function of worm and lover is the same. The engines of the "old arsenal" of love are "crime, horror, folly," and they are brought to bear in "the hell of your bed." For love "is a crime in which one cannot do without an accomplice." Love is criminal; it bears the stain of mortal sin which cannot be eradicated even in the most disciplined and serene of conjugal relations. "In love, as in almost all human affairs, *l'entente cordiale* is the result of a misunderstanding. This misunderstanding is pleasure. The man cries: 'O my angel!' The woman coos and warbles. And these two imbeciles are persuaded that they think in concert.—The uncrossable gulf, which is the cause of incommunicability, remains uncrossed." The love relation is a manacle masquerading as pleasure: "Like a convict to his chain, like the helpless gambler to the game, like the drunkard to his bottle, like the vermin to the corpse, I am tied to you who make of my humiliated spirit your bed and your demesne." One partner is vampire and executioner; the other is victim.

Baudelaire not only presents love in terms of death, but presents death with all the allure of a woman dressed for a ball, in "Danse Macabre":

D'une coquette maigre, aux airs extravagants . . .
Vit-on jamais au bal une taille plus mince?
        . . . un pied sec que pince
Un soulier pomponné, joli comme une fleur . . .
L'élégance sans nom de l'humaine armature.

A thin coquette, with extravagant airs . . .
Did one ever see at the ball a thinner waist?
        . . . a dry foot which
A pomponned slipper, pretty as a flower, pinches . . .
The nameless elegance of the human armature.

Above the scene of the danse macabre one sees:

Dans un trou du plafond la trompette de l'Ange
Sinistrement béante ainsi qu'un tromblon noir.

In a hole in the ceiling the trumpet of the Angel
Sinisterly gaping like a black blunderbuss.

The skeleton is dressed in the vanities of this world; the Angel waits above the ballroom to sound on the Last Day the trump of doom, which for the sinner is a blunderbuss whose barrel is curved outwards at the end like that of a trumpet.

Just as the skeleton can take on the parure of living flesh, that same living flesh can disintegrate into first a wineskin, symbol of brutish appetition, and then into a skeleton. This appears in "Les Métamorphoses du Vampire." The woman, as symbolic vampire of lust, has drawn from him all she desires:

—Quand elle eut de mes os sucé toute la moelle,
Et que languissamment je me tournai vers elle
Pour lui rendre un baiser d'amour, je ne vis plus
Qu'un outre aux flancs gluants, toute pleine de pus!

—When she had sucked all the marrow from my bones
And when I turned languidly toward her
To give her a loving kiss, I saw
Only a wineskin with sticky sides, quite full of pus!

And when he looks again, in the place of the wineskin *tremblaient confusement des débris de squelette*—the debris of a skeleton was trembling confusedly.

In "Une Charogne," a violent inventory of the process of bodily decomposition takes the place of the conventional poetic reflection or elegy on mortality. The relationship between love and death is clearly stressed. The worm "will eat you with kisses," performing the same function as the lover. The corpse appears to recline like a lustful woman. The palace of love will soon become the burrow of worms— a conventional figure.

Ironically, the corpse is seen on a *beau matin d'été si doux*—a fine, gentle summer morning. The language and figures of speech describing the decomposition have a joyful precision and exuberance in rendering the scene so well. Through the lens of the artist, the horrible object has become beautiful in that its transference through the medium of figures of speech has been so successful that we are attracted to the display and execution of the poet's craft. "It is one of the prodigious privileges of art that the horrible, artistically expressed, becomes beauty. What is beautiful is no more decent than indecent."

The achievement of a beautiful poem—that is, one that exhibits technical proficiency, skill in the use of figures of speech and so on—is indifferent to whether the poem is civil, polite, and decent, or not. "Une Charogne" is by many standards impolite and indecent. It is certainly not immoral. It reminds us of what artificial politeness and decency invite us to forget, when they lead us to take up residence in an abstraction from the concrete whole of experience. The corpse, charogne infâme,

> Les jambes en l'air, comme une femme lubrique,
> > Brûlante et suant les poisons,
> Ouvrait d'une façon nonchalante et cynique
> > Son ventre pleine d'exhalaisons.

> Legs in the air, like a lustful woman,
> > Roasting and sweating poisons,
> Opened nonchalantly and cynically
> > Its belly full of exhalations.

Ironically the stiff posture of death is that of lust also. Ironically, the corpse, like a lewd and crass harlot, displays its rotting entrails, in proud and contemptuous defiance— nonchalante et cynique—of the refinements and conventions of her betters.

> . . . la carcasse superbe
> Comme une fleur s'épanouir.

Here is a Fleur du Mal, paradoxically a flower, blooming and richly expanding, but at the same time a mass of corruption. "Une Charogne" uses superbe to indicate the rapid, parasitic efflorescence of life in the corpse, blooming explosively, proudly attracting all attention.

Baudelaire perhaps owes his interest in the physical horror of death and decomposition to Gautier. He says in praise of him: "When a grotesque or hideous object offered itself to his eyes, he knew how to extract even from it a mysterious and symbolic beauty." Gautier's use of language and imagery is less vivid than Baudelaire's:

Ta chair délicate et superbe
Va servir de pâture aux vers.[1]

Your delicate and superb flesh
Will go to serve as a pasture of worms.

"Une Charogne" develops a group of associations which completely enclose the decaying body. These associations develop a pressure which is increased as each metaphor is added until the description has been completely sealed up, intact, with all holes stopped by the proper imagery. Thus, as the poem builds up its pressure, each image delivers more and more impact, depending upon its predecessors for support and extending them. This may account for the way these lines compel our attention:

> . . . sur ce ventre putride,
> D'où sortaient de noirs bataillons
> De larves qui coulaient comme un épais liquide
> Le long de ces vivants haillons.

> Tout cela descendait, montait comme une vague,
> Ou s'élançait en pétillant; . . .

> . . . on this putrid belly
> From whence came dark battalions
> Of larvae, who flowed like a thick liquid
> Along these living tatters and rags.

> All that descended, mounted like a wave,
> Or rushed itself along, crackling; . . .

Cumulatively, the image extends itself, building up pressure. Sound is introduced. The mass of worms *s'élançaient en pétillant*—rushed while crackling—with strange music like

---

[1] Théophile Gautier, "Les Affres de la Mort." Edgar Allan Poe also certainly contributed. But Poe never developed beyond the machinery of horror. He wanted to develop in his poems that "frisson" which Hugo loved to present and which Hugo thought was Baudelaire's greatest merit.

"the grain that a winnower agitates and turns in his winnow."

The apostrophe *Et pourtant vous serez semblable à cette ordure* is grandiose, baroque, but effective enough with its broad rhetorical impetus and rhythmical swing. It is conventionally handled and the convention is a dependable one.

The relationship between lust and death is likewise, in "Un Voyage à Cythère," centered around the process of physical decomposition, the putrescence of flesh. The poem is introduced in the conversational-ironic tone, the tone of Jules Laforgue. A voyage is being made to Cythera, the Venusberg and traditional island paradise of lust:

> Quelle est cette île triste et noire?—C'est Cythère,
> Nous dit-on, un pays fameux dans les chansons,
> Eldorado banal de tous les vieux garçons.
> Regardez, après tout, c'est une pauvre terre.

> What is this sad dark island?—It is Cythera,
> We are told, a country famous in the songs,
> Banal Eldorado of all the old playboys.
> Look, after all, it's a poor place.

This stanza seems to me to contain the most successful example of Baudelaire's irony. The island of Watteau, the dream of the eighteenth century, the *fêtes galantes* which attracted Verlaine's poetry, are damned with the greatest anathema which the generation of Flaubert and Baudelaire could hurl. They are *banal*; they are the haunt and sojourn of *tous les vieux garçons*—the old goats of the Jockey Club, or the comfortably-off retired bourgeois when they can escape from wife and family for an evening. Cythera no longer has the allure of sin; it is the custom, the convention; it is another *café* or *moulin* on the boulevards and is haunted by banal boulevardiers. What a disappointment! *Regardez, après tout, c'est une pauvre terre.*

Baudelaire is strongly opposed to the art of Cythera—of Watteau and of Verlaine, or of Mendelssohn. In his essay on Gautier he states:

"Up to an advanced enough point in modern times, art, poetry, and music especially have had as an aim only to enchant the spirit in presenting it with pictures of bliss, contrasting with the horrible life of contention and struggle in which we are plunged.

"Beethoven began to stir up the worlds of melancholy and incurable despair amassed like clouds in the interior sky of man. Byron and Poe—the one, in spite of his prolixity and his verbiage, so detestably imitated by Alfred de Musset; the other, in spite of his irritating concision—have expressed the blasphemous part of passion; they have projected splendid rays on the latent Lucifer who is installed in every human heart."

This is in some ways the usual Romantic protest, with its appeal to Byron and Poe. But Baudelaire does not follow it in the direction of forced melodrama, antithesis, the raging waters around the jagged cliff, or the swarthy hero exiled by society. He is reacting against the art of Watteau and of Musset and Lamartine—art which ignores paradox and denies the Devil.

Baudelaire is on the side of Beethoven. After the ironical passage, the central image of the poem appears:

J'entrevoyais pourtant un objet singulier, . . .
Nous vîmes que c'était un gibet à trois branches,
Du ciel se détachant en noir, comme un cyprès.

De féroces oiseaux perchés sur leur pâture
Détruisaient avec rage un pendu déjà mûr,
Chacun plantant, comme un outil, son bec impur
Dans tous les coins saignants de cette pourriture;

Les yeux étaient deux trous, et du ventre effondré
Les intestins pesants lui coulaient sur les cuisses,
Et ses bourreaux, gorgés de hideuses délices,
L'avaient à coups de bec absolument châtré.

I glimpsed nevertheless a singular object, . . .
We saw that it was a three-branched gibbet,
Standing out in black against the sky, like a cypress.

Ferocious birds perched on their food
Destroyed with rage a hanged man who was already ripe,
Each one planting his corrupt beak like a tool
In all the bleeding corners of this rottenness;

The eyes were two holes, and from the broken-open belly
The heavy intestines flowed over his thighs,
And his executioners, gorged with hideous delights,
Had completely emasculated him with their beaks.

Watteau shows us "The Embarkation for Cythera," the preliminary gallantry and flirtation. Baudelaire shows us what awaits the gallants when they arrive at the island itself, which island Watteau only hints at. Not only is the island (the act of lust) a disappointment—*Regardez, après tout, c'est une pauvre terre*—but it is a punishment for the pleasure with which it allures the victim.

Here is the same interest in putrefaction that was observed in "Une Charogne." Indulgence in lust has torn the body to pieces. Lust feeds upon him, beginning with its own special parts, rather than providing him pleasure. He is at the mercy of the beaks, which, like tools—*outils*, skillfully dismember him. Death and lust are inextricably fused. The passage from "Fusées," III, is still of interest: "Love resembles strongly a torture or a surgical operation. . . . Do you hear these sighs . . . these moans, these cries, these death rattles? . . . And the human face relaxes itself in a sort of death. For surely I would commit a sacrilege in applying the word 'ecstasy' to this kind of decomposition." So difficult is it in this life to keep the body a temple to its creator, so easy is its abuse, that the poem ends, sincerely I think, with a religious appeal:

—Ah! Seigneur! donnez-moi la force et le courage
De contempler mon cœur et mon corps sans dégoût!

—Ah! Lord! give me the strength and the courage
To contemplate my heart and my body without disgust!

Baudelaire cannot see earthly love as a symbol of divine
love, as Dante did in his Beatrice. For Baudelaire, Beatrice
symbolizes only lust-love. Man's sin has poisoned every
aspect of the love relationship which should ideally be a
re-enactment of God's love to man. Baudelaire, in the poem
"La Béatrice," presents himself as a Dante who sees, while
he wanders through Inferno, his divine Beatrice fornicating
with goat-legged demons and laughing at him the while.

LA BÉATRICE

Dans des terrains cendreux, calcinés, sans verdure,
Comme je me plaignais un jour à la nature,
Et que de ma pensée, en vaguant au hasard,
J'aiguisais lentement sur mon cœur le poignard,
Je vis en plein midi descendre sur ma tête
Un nuage funèbre et gros d'une tempête,
Qui portait un troupeau de démons vicieux,
Semblables à des nains cruels et curieux.
A me considérer froidement ils se mirent,
Et, comme des passants sur un fou qu'ils admirent,
Je les entendis rire et chuchoter entre eux,
En échangeant maint signe et maint clignement d'yeux:

—"Contemplons à loisir cette caricature
Et cette ombre d'Hamlet imitant sa posture,
Le regard indécis et les cheveux au vent.
N'est-ce pas grand'pitié de voir ce bon vivant,
Ce gueux, cet histrion en vacances, ce drôle,
Parce qu'il sait jouer artistement son rôle,
Vouloir intéresser au chant de ses douleurs
Les aigles, les grillons, les ruisseaux et les fleurs,
Et même à nous, auteurs de ces vieilles rubriques,
Réciter en hurlant ses tirades publiques?"

J'aurais pu (mon orgueil aussi haut que les monts
Domine la nuée et le cri des démons)
Détourner simplement ma tête souveraine,
Si je n'eusse pas vu parmi leur troupe obscène
Crime qui n'a pas fait chanceler le soleil!
La reine de mon cœur, au regard nonpareil,
Qui riait avec eux de ma sombre détresse
Et leur versait parfois quelque sale caresse.

BEATRICE

In terrains covered with ashes, calcined, without verdure,
As I lamented one day to nature
And as I sharpened slowly on my heart
The poignard of my thought which wandered about at
    random,
I saw at full noon descend over my head
The large ominous cloud of a tempest,
Which carried a flock of vicious demons,
Resembling cruel and inquisitive dwarfs.
They began to examine me coldly
And, like passers-by about a lunatic at whom they are
    astonished,
I heard them laugh and whisper among themselves
While exchanging many a sign and wink of the eye:

—"Let us contemplate at leisure this caricature
And this shadow of Hamlet, imitating Hamlet's posture,
With his irresolute glance and his hair in the wind.
Is it not a great pity to see this jolly fellow,
This beggar, this second-rate actor on a vacation, this
    scamp,
Because he knows how to play his role artistically,
Wish to interest in the singing of his sorrows
The eagles, the crickets, the streams, and the flowers,
And even recite, howling, his public tirades,
To us, authors as we are of those old rubrics?"

I might have (my pride as high as the mountains
Dominates the numerous cloud of the demons and their
    cry)
Turned my sovereign head away simply
If I had not seen among their obscene troop
Crime which did not make the sun totter!
The queen of my heart, she of the unparalleled gaze,
Who laughed with them at my somber distress
And poured out to them at times some filthy caress.

The "terrains, covered with ashes, calcined" are those of
Inferno certainly. Baudelaire has treated the situation with
the irony of a Laforgue. He ridicules himself in the guise
of a Romantic's Hamlet. The vicious demons appear to be
merely mischievous; we laugh with them at the brooding,
sulking hero's expense. We are carried over into the witty
demons' faction, for even at the end, the hero is striking a
pose: "My pride as high as the mountains dominates the
numerous cloud of the demons and their cry." But we are
shocked suddenly by realizing that we have been on the
wrong side, when we read the final lines.

These demons are vicious; they have corrupted the pure
Beatrice beloved by the poet. Their ingenious mockery,
when viewed from the conclusion of the poem, seems merely
to accentuate their evil. They are vicious, like clever children prematurely old in the practice of depravity. We have
come so close to being taken in by their scornful cleverness
that the impact of the concluding image of the filthy caress
is a moral lesson which we have discovered ourselves. Baudelaire has said elsewhere that the spirit of irony and mockery
is rarely compatible with charity: "Irony—satanic turn of
the spirit." Mockery can conceal evil as Beatrice or any
other woman can conceal "the eternal Venus—one of the
seductive disguises of the devil."

7

It is part of Baudelaire's achievement that he managed
to combine this dangerous irony, exhibited in "La Béatrice,"
with charity in many of his poems. In doing so he has
strengthened both for poetic use. Unsupported irony approaches a display of wit alone. Unsupported charity is
endangered by sentimentality, the reliance on feeling alone.
When the two are harnessed, or locked together, they are
mutually supporting. And in such a poem as "La servante
au grand cœur dont vous étiez jalouse" it is impossible to
unlock them because no one can find the seam at which
they were joined. Irony flows freely through the arteries of
this poem's structure and so does charity. We cannot distinguish one from another, they are one bloodstream. Certainly their origination was simultaneous and unpremedi-
tated; Baudelaire developed them as a unity, as an integer.

The poem concerns the beloved nurse, now long dead,
of his happy childhood.

> La servante au grand cœur dont vous étiez jalouse,
> Et qui dort son sommeil sous une humble pelouse,
> Nous devrions pourtant lui porter quelques fleurs.
> Les morts, les pauvres morts, ont de grandes douleurs,
> Et quand Octobre souffle, émondeur des vieux arbres,
> Son vent mélancolique à l'entour de leurs marbres,
> Certe, ils doivent trouver les vivants bien ingrats,
> A dormir, comme ils font, chaudement dans leurs draps,
> Tandis que, dévorés de noires songeries,
> Sans compagnon de lit, sans bonnes causeries,
> Vieux squelettes gelés travaillés par le ver,
> Ils sentent s'égoutter les neiges de l'hiver

Et le siècle couler, sans qu'amis ni famille
Remplacent les lambeaux qui pendent à leur grille.

Lorsque la bûche siffle et chante, si le soir,
Calme, dans le fauteuil je la voyais s'asseoir,
Si, par une nuit bleue et froide de décembre,
Je la trouvais tapie en un coin de ma chambre,
Grave, et venant du fond de son lit éternel
Couver l'enfant grandi de son œil maternel,
Que pourrais-je répondre à cette âme pieuse,
Voyant tomber des pleurs de sa paupière creuse?

The great-hearted servant of whom you were jealous,
And who sleeps her sleep under a humble grass plot,
We should nevertheless bring her some flowers.
The dead, the poor dead, have great sorrows,
And when October, that pruner of old trees,
Blows his melancholy wind around their marble slabs,
Surely they must find the living very ungrateful
To sleep, as they do, warmly between their sheets
While, devoured by dark reveries,
Without a bed-companion, without a good chance to chat,
Old frozen skeletons worked over by the worm,
They feel the snows of winter draining through the ground
And the century flowing along, while neither friends nor
    family
Replace the shreds which hang from their grating.

If while the burning log whistles and sings, in the evening,
I saw her sit down calm in the armchair,
If, on a blue and cold night in December,
I found her curled up in a corner of my room,
Grave, and coming from the depth of her eternal bed
To gaze on the grown child with her maternal eye,
What could I answer to this pious soul,
Seeing the tears fall from her hollow eyelid?

Irony here has infused charity. The slyness of presentation, the playful entries, the half-serious tone, bring us in to the poem and bring us imperceptibly to a climax of emotive feeling, the great strength and compulsion of which lies in its restraint. Sympathy and feeling have been conveyed without sentimentality. Irony is the edge of sympathy in this poem; it both sharpens the power of the feeling implicit in the poem, and at the same time provides a walled edge beyond which the poem cannot go. Irony has limited the area of the poem; it has eliminated and disciplined, narrowing down the material which can be used. The effect of concentration obtained by restraint is added to the dramatic paradoxical effect of the conjunction of irony and sympathy. The irony is no mere vehicle which we use to take us into the poem and which we then discard. Its metallic threads are woven throughout the texture, shining even against the black velvet of the conclusion. These threads are worked with deft turns around the principal chords of the poem, forming an obbligato which is their necessary complement.

The poet is witty in this poem, but his wit is humbly and gently infused. He laughs with humility; for he is awed by his old nurse. The style is style *soleil couchant*, suffused with the soft tints of its humor, with its gravity and sureness of movement, its rhythm, and the accuracy of its cadences.

We enter the poem casually. Mention has been made of the old servant—"You must remember her—she is the one who died some time ago—she was

La servante au grand cœur dont vous étiez jalouse.

The great-hearted servant· of whom you were jealous.

Poor old thing! We should perhaps take her *quelques fleurs*." The *quelques fleurs* is here the emblem of conventional sentiment. If you have an old dead servant whom you have forgotten, atone for your heedlessness by bringing her "some flowers." The conversational tone, almost that of

Laforgue, prevails. The servant is a poor old thing—the object of conventional pity. She possibly means no more to the poet than old Françoise did to Flaubert. Baudelaire's servant could be regarded only as a *cœur simple*. Yet for all her simplicity and his gentle laughter, he proclaims her *grand cœur* by his tenderness, by his respect for her wisdom.

Les morts, les pauvres morts, ont de grandes douleurs.

The dead, the poor dead, have great sorrows.

It is again a conventional remark. She is so unhappy where she is now! And it is an ironical remark, for it is just the kind of a remark the good-hearted old nurse would have made whenever she thought of a dead friend. The dead have *douleurs*—they are unhappy, that is her idea of death. When Baudelaire speaks in his own voice about the dead, they are

Vieux squelettes gelés travaillés par le ver.

Old frozen skeletons worked over by the worm.

The nurse would never have thought of this. But even those macabre details are *lovingly* applied; they are domesticated so that they may enter the poem. He does not wish to frighten either us or the old nurse; he wishes to convey to us the bond between his sorrow and hers and ours.

October is the *émondeur de vieux arbres*—pruner of old trees—a pathetic image, since October makes old people uncomfortable. They feel like old trees being pruned of their leaves, because they are reminded of approaching death. The implied connection between the old servant and the autumn trees provides the first major ripple of feeling in the poem. Again, Baudelaire implies that the dead are their own tombstones, huddled together in the cemetery, complaining softly of the intrusion of the wind upon their conclave. Even more than by her own physical discomfort, the old nurse is upset by the impoliteness of the living. *Certes*, they have bad manners, they are *bien ingrats* in not remembering her services.

For the dead do without the good things of life. The good things in life—they are, she knows, *bonnes causeries* (good chats), a warm *compagnon de lit* (she dislikes ever being alone), and freedom from *noires songeries* (dark reveries). Baudelaire presents her desires ironically, knowing how dear to himself are those same *noires songeries* and how unsatisfactory for him are the *compagnons de lit* and the *bonnes causeries*. Yet he laments the loss which his servant has endured. Who knows, perhaps the satisfactions she needs are the equipment of a higher wisdom, which he cannot penetrate or guess. His laughter is affectionate; the domesticated macabre details, the *vieux squelettes gelés*, are lovingly applied, like arabesques, or musical ornamentation. *Le siècle coule*—the century flows—taking all this with it, and we arrive at a cadence, a stop, a partial resolution:

> *Et le siècle couler, sans qu'amis ni famille*
> *Remplacent les lambeaux qui pendent à leur grille.*

> And the century flowing along, while neither friends nor family
> Replace the shreds which hang from their grating.

Where will he go from here? We have had a similar stoppage in line four, where

> *Les morts, les pauvres morts, ont de grandes douleurs*

formed the cadence. October, however, took up the theme and developed the *douleurs*—the sorrows of our servant. The present stoppage, however, has completed the arrangement of the nurse's character and point of view as viewed by an affectionate humorist. To go beyond this stage of development, Baudelaire must of course maintain the tone of his first section and bring round to a new track the same curve which he has just brought to rest. This is easy for him to do; he can start again in many directions.

The second section proceeds to tie the nurse in closely to Baudelaire's heart and to his problems. Her memory becomes for him intense and present; it accuses him, as if her death and her subterranean discomforts were his own fault. October gives way to a night-blue December, a room in his mind where she appears.

> Que pourrais-je répondre à cette âme pieuse,
> Voyant tomber des pleurs de sa paupière creuse?

> What could I answer to this pious soul,
> Seeing the tears fall from her hollow eyelid?

What can the subtle, sophisticated poet, the enfant grandi, say before the simple, gravely serious old woman who has come to watch her "grown-up child" and to take in his cleverness, like a stolid peasant who watches a juggler at the county fair but is not convinced by his prodigious gyrations. The wisdom of the simple old woman is durable in contrast to his sallies, his attempts, his momentary captures. Grave and maternal, the old woman is pieuse; she weeps on account of her miseries underground and on account of the misery of the child she had nursed, but her religious faith is unquestioned. Que pourrais-je répondre? He can tell her nothing about life and death; he cannot explain the change which she has had to undergo. She has won; her wisdom is strong; her power over his heart is strong. And yet the brassy thread of irony glints against her darkness: she is pieuse as Flaubert's Françoise is pieuse; her unshakable peasant faith is surrounded on its visible surface by superstition.

The tension between irony and sympathy has sharpened both, endowing the poem with its power. This luminous irony is distinct from the wit of Donne or Marvell. They tend to develop a situation which can be efficiently exploited for the development of ingenious metaphor, counterbalances, and paradoxes. In doing so, they frequently develop great power, great undershadowing of and oblique reference to the major paradoxes. The vehicle, a convention such as the relation of love to mortality in "To His Coy Mistress," is a forethought; a means of getting into the poet's mind. The fertility of this mind then proceeds to exhaust the conventional vehicle of so much association and implication that it tears us "with rough strife/Through the iron gates of life." The action of wit then, the *tour de force*, is with Donne and Marvell to develop the conventional vehicle until it embraces the "iron gates" through which all the subtleties and complexities of their minds are arranged.

The irony of Baudelaire, however, is an undertone. It develops the theme and it provides counterpoint for it, but it does not subsume the theme. We have examples of Baudelaire in the metaphysical style:

> *Nos deux cœurs seront deux vastes flambeaux*
> *Qui refléchiront leurs doubles lumières*
> *Dans nos deux esprits, ces miroirs jumeaux.*

> *Our two hearts will be two large torches*
> *Which will reflect their double lights*
> *In our two spirits, those twin mirrors.*

He tended on the whole to utilize such wit infrequently. But he revives the seventeenth century English poets' brilliant use of metaphor. They build their structure from metaphor to metaphor, keeping the whole span or bridge tied at both ends to land by using the conventional vehicle which also bolts the related images together. Baudelaire's imagery, by contrast, seems to be drawn up out of the ground; his poem forms a solid embankment or causeway, rather than a suspension bridge.

Baudelaire's irony must be further differentiated from that of Webster. Webster is full of echoes. Webster's mocking laugh echoes up and down the soiled marble halls, like that of the Marlowe of *The Jew of Malta*, or the Shakespeare of *Troilus and Cressida*. Webster and Baudelaire depended alike on the conventional macabre, the stock horror imagery. But in Webster the macabre is interesting; after a while it becomes terrifying. The skull is really riding close behind the skin-clad face. Baudelaire adds the crossbones to the skull; he plays a game; he imitates a pirate or a skeleton and juggles their familiar emblems before us. *Une odeur de tombeau dans les ténèbres nage*—a smell of the tomb floats in the shadows—and so forth. (Remember his stories of his trip to Africa "and Calcutta." Calcutta must be a very strange place, scarcely earthly. It is, no doubt, inhabited by crustaceans.) Webster's irony is no ambitious suspension bridge, but, like Baudelaire's, runs along the foundations of his work. Its integration with the whole produces the magnificent Websterian echoes which are in essence mockery.

The murder of the Duchess of Malfi in Webster's play is a conspiracy to which every action, every speech within the play, however innocent, contributes and reverberates. It is a burlesque on total depravity of human nature, cruel, mocking, true, and false. Even Vittoria Corombona's speech in *The White Devil* is a burlesque. The question is: What are the facings we can place before the evil within us, not really to justify ourselves, but merely to pass the time, as Bosola assassinated to pass the time?

Baudelaire, on the other hand, possesses cœur. The poem about his old nurse is the greatest example of the mature splendor and restrained emotion of cœur. He avoids mockery in his poetry (but not in his prose). Cœur is akin to sympathy, to emotive feeling. It is a movement both physiological and psychological, partaking somewhat of the moral impulse and closely akin to it. It is not to be mistaken for an ecstasy or exhilaration. It is the gateway to peace. We must remember that Baudelaire regards himself and his fellows as victims, victims of sin and of modern metropolitan civilization. Again Baudelaire associates the aesthetic and the moral impulses, the city offending both.

How does the heart fare in this labyrinth? How does it contract, how does it flare up, how does it expand with the peace of the balcony sunset? *Que les soleils sont beaux dans les chaudes soirées!* How beautiful the suns are in the warm evenings! The heart is symbol of love and peace that are possible and of anguish that is present. The metropolitan background varies in these poems of remorse and anguish, explicit in some, implicit in others. Irony is part of the sinews of this heart, too, providing a framework, a girder system which resists sentimentality.

We have already discussed the heart of Célimène—the withered, desiccated heart of self-esteem and superciliousness.[1] Her heart is mummified, a carcass from which the living fluid has been drained—*cœur racorni, fumé comme un jambon*—shriveled heart, smoked like a ham. We have also considered the symbolic completion of the mature heart's life cycle:

Quand notre cœur a une fois fait sa vendange.[2]

Baudelaire's nurse is also the servant *au grand cœur.*

This luminous red weight in the breast integrates us and draws us into spiritual movement. Many times, the sun appears as a contributory image to the heart, supporting it. The *cœur* symbol subsumes *soleil*, thus strengthening itself.

"Chant d'Automne" has a metropolitan scene. Cœur and its supporting *soleil* are suspended in it. The heart is betraying itself; its latent warmth and sympathy are given up and its ruddy mass solidifies as a frozen cube in this poem.

CHANT D'AUTOMNE

Bientôt nous plongerons dans les froides ténèbres;
Adieu, vive clarté de nos étés trop courts!
J'entends déjà tomber avec des chocs funèbres
Le bois retentissant sur le pavé des cours.

Tout l'hiver va rentrer dans mon être: colère,
Haine, frissons, horreur, labeur dur et forcé,

[1] Cf. pp. 45-46 above.
[2] Cf. pp. 36-37 above.

Et, comme le soleil dans son enfer polaire,
Mon cœur ne sera plus qu'un bloc rouge et glacé.

J'écoute en frémissant chaque bûche qui tombe;
L'échafaud qu'on bâtit n'a pas d'écho plus sourd.
Mon esprit est pareil à la tour qui succombe
Sous les coups du bélier infatigable et lourd.

Il me semble, bercé par ce choc monotone,
Qu'on cloue en grande hâte un cercueil quelque part.
Pour qui?—C'était hier l'été; voici l'automne!
Ce bruit mystérieux sonne comme un départ.

SONG OF AUTUMN

Soon we will plunge into the cold shadows;
Adieu, vivid clearness of our too-short summers!
I already hear the wood resounding
On the courtyard pavement with mournful shocks.

All of winter is going to return within me: anger
Hatred, shudders, horror, hard and forced labor,
And like the sun in his polar hell,
My heart will be only a red and frozen block.

Trembling I hear each log which falls;
A scaffold being raised has the same dull and heavy echo.
My spirit is like the tower which succumbs
Under the blows of the heavy and indefatigable ram.

It seems to me, lulled by this monotonous shock,
That somewhere they are nailing up a coffin in great
    haste.
For whom?—Yesterday was summer; here is autumn!
This mysterious sound tolls as for a departure.

"Chant d'Automne" is possessed by the noise of falling
wood. An end has come; the season has died. The recurrence
of decay in the annual seasonal cycle, caught up in this
sound, reverberates through the heart:

J'entends déjà tomber avec des chocs funèbres
Le bois retentissant sur le pavé des cours.

I already hear the wood resounding
On the courtyard pavement with mournful shocks.

The scene is still beautiful: courtyards being piled with logs; we can imagine trees in the background, their leaves changing color. The season is closing in on Baudelaire with walls of fog:

Bientôt nous plongerons dans les froids ténèbres.

Soon we will plunge into the cold shadows.

Noises, smells, somber colors which he had forgotten for a brief season are unexpectedly brought before him by this singular noise of autumn, *ce choc monotone.* Like Proust's involuntary memory, this one mysterious sound evokes a chain of associated sensations, all melancholy:

Tout l'hiver va rentrer dans mon être.

All of winter is going to return within me.

As each day advances, he must return more and more to his winter slavery to *colère, haine, frissons, horreur, labeur dur et forcé*—anger, hatred, shudders, horror, hard and forced labor. He will fight a losing battle against them; his tower will succumb. The noise of the wood suggests that a coffin is being built and that a scaffolding is being raised; he must offer himself as sacrifice to the violent humors of the metropolitan winter. The summer has given him a glimpse of peace and harmony, the possible serenity that taunts him in his delinquency:

Adieu, vive clarté de nos étés trop courts!

Adieu, vivid clearness of our too-short summers!

The winter is of course the symbol of his falling away into pride, fear, and hatred. His anguish comes from his glimpse of summer, from its possibility. He alone is to blame for his slavery to sin. He suffers hatred, terror, and fear because he follows egotism and desire. To carry this mass of corruption along with him from day to day is *labeur dur et forcé*.

J'écoute en frémissant chaque bûche qui tombe;
L'échafaud qu'on bâtit n'a pas d'écho plus sourd.

Trembling I hear each log which falls;
A scaffold being raised has the same dull and heavy echo.

The noise of falling wood has touched off the train of sensations which detonate desire and pride. These together attack his tower in the form of a battering ram.

Et comme le soleil dans son enfer polaire,
Mon cœur ne sera plus qu'un bloc rouge et glacé.

And like the sun in his polar hell,
My heart will be only a red and frozen block.

We observe that Baudelaire does not baldly state his feeling by saying "My heart is cold," as Shelley, Hugo, Musset, and Lamartine would have. Baudelaire has set himself the problem of actualization: he seeks in the physical realm that correspondent of his emotional state which will bring his state *concretely* before the reader. To call the heart "cold" would be to present the state *abstractly*, merely assigning it a conventional name or sign. But the red and frozen block, the polar sun setting in a red blaze, combined with the poignancy of the cyclical seasonal change, causes the reader to enter into the labor of the poem. As Baudelaire put it: "In the written word, there is always a gap completed by the imagination of the hearer."

This completion of the gap by the reader is the way in which a poem gives knowledge. It awakens the reader to correspondences and relationships which he not only seems to discover but actually does discover for himself, because he must himself bridge the gap by testing the comparison to see if it is valid for his experience. The polar sun sinking in his flamboyant sunset, as if into an icy hell, must be translated to the heart which is sensitive to the decay of the season. Formerly warm and quick-blooded with sympathy and love, as if in summer, the heart begins to freeze, with the first hints of winter, into pride, fear, hatred, and desire, which are all pride fundamentally. The heart, warm and live as it functions physically, becomes, under pride and desire, a frozen red cube. It stains the vast empty plateaus of ice with its polar sunset. It emits no heat, but light only, and that dark red and purplish. Boreal twilight coldly beaconed by a dark red star in the shape of a cube is the hibernation of the heart, glowing only in memory of summer clarity of unselfishness and love. The heart as frozen cube and the heart as incandescent sun represent the opposite solstices of its cyclical change.

The autumn twilight is a part of the metropolitan background. The victim bears his heart as if in his outstretched hands. With it luminous before him, he cannot forget the love and peace that are possible even in the metropolis. And even when its glow is nearly extinct, the heart causes all his pain and anguish, remembering what is possible. The heart remembers: *Quel éloignement!* Time and spleen torture it with memory of lost opportunities for regeneration, and anger of spite and pride. City scenes surround it with misery and force from it, as if treading juice from grapes, all its vintage of pity for suffering.

Time is one of the rulers of metropolis. The clock, "L'Horloge" of the poem of that name, strictly marks the growth of the past. It reminds that the past grows as loss and waste.

> *Trois mille six cents fois par heure, la Seconde*
> *Chuchote: Souviens-toi!—Rapide, avec sa voix*
> *D'insecte, Maintenant dit: Je suis Autrefois,*
> *Et j'ai pompé ta vie avec ma trompe immonde!*

Three thousand six hundred times an hour, the Second
Whispers: Remember!—Rapid with his voice
Of an insect, Now says: I am Formerly, I am Past,
And I have eaten up your life with my unclean insect's
    snout.

A common philosophic observation—the present constantly becomes the past. But the clock is a memorial to this continual loss. It will not allow one to forget that life is being wasted. The voice of the clock is whispery, swift, and unvarying. Its tick is the noise of an insect rasping his feelers together. The cruel expansion of this comparison with an insect is the development of a nose, a proboscis for it, with which it eats up a man's life. In what is left of one's life, as in the past:

Les vibrantes Douleurs dans ton cœur plein d'effroi
Se planteront bientôt comme dans une cible.

Vibrant sorrows in your heart full of terror
Will fix themselves soon as in a target.

The melancholy hero attracts all sorrows. This is an exaggerated statement, but the image is good. The hero feels his heart is a target; it is moreover vaguely similar in shape. The sorrows are arrows that vibrate after fixing themselves in it. Sorrow may be said to be vibrant; it occurs in spasms. So that the heart shakes with sharp waves of anguish whose vibrations subside until they do not occur periodically but merge into a steady dull pain. Likewise the arrow shakes and vibrates after planting itself in a target until it finally rests quietly with its barb firmly seated in the center.

    Le Plaisir vaporeux fuira vers l'horizon
    Ainsi qu'une sylphide au fond de la coulisse.

    Vaporous pleasure will flee towards the horizon
    Like a sylph at the back of the side-scene.

In the future as in the past, sadness will come and pleasure will flee. Pleasure is unreal and vaporous. Whenever we approach it, it retreats a corresponding distance toward the horizon. It actually does not exist; it is merely represented as a sylph or wood nymph is represented on the stage. As long as you abide by the convention and pretend that the stage is real life, you can suppose that pleasure exists and watch it while you are seated in the audience. But you cannot grasp it yourself; you cannot be one of the actors. If you jump up on the stage to seize it, the sylph will evaporate into the side-scenes, into the wings of the stage. This depth of implication exists in the one seemingly simple simile.

We observe that Baudelaire often employs the standard situations of his immediate predecessors, as in the case of the melancholy man who attracts all sorrows. He generally bothers, however, to actualize the emotion, in this case with the target and arrows.

The poem is about time; thirty-six hundred times a minute the seconds whisper their warning by the clock. The minutes are matrices which must be cracked so that their gold may be extracted.

Le jour décroît; la nuit augmente; souviens-toi!
Le gouffre a toujours soif; la clepsydre se vide.

The day grows shorter; night increases; remember!
The gulf is always athirst; the water-clock is emptying.

Like Marvell, the poet attempts to establish the passage of time with examples from the world. But while his examples are less striking, Baudelaire communicates the sense of loss involved in time past, with which Marvell's "To His Coy Mistress" and MacLeish's "You, Andrew Marvell" do not deal. Those poems present the onrush and ineluctable change of time with the winged chariot and the turning of earth's globe. When placed beside the comparisons with which those fine poems have involved time, Baudelaire's simple metaphors are less effective: day grows short; night increases; the water-clock empties. Yet with the one phrase *souviens-toi* we have entered a world removed from that of other poets. Marvell and MacLeish have watched time from vast distances and vast panoramas—deserts of vast eternity—and have seen the planet turning far beneath them.

With Baudelaire we return to the imagined metropolis which is, for the mind, a stuffy microcosm, a room with a street outside, and a street lamp. Baudelaire's *souviens-toi* brings us to the sense of loss; we feel that time is a steady cancer methodically blighting the areas, the bulk and masses of the mind, sinking in and rotting it away on schedule until only a small sound portion remains to be devoured. Time consumes; for the past is waste; pride and desire corrupt every moment of it. The memory of the tumor which is the past is intolerable. The anticipation of the minutes and seconds yet to come is intolerable. For this reason, each second that comes up in the present is likewise wastefully consumed in an attempt to achieve forgetfulness of past and future by distraction. Each present second is stored away a burned-out husk, to be counted up into the past.

Dread of the future and shame for the past can only be overcome by love (that is, by Christian *agape*, not pagan *eros*). It is written that one should never be troubled about tomorrow; tomorrow will take care of itself. But if the present is expended in egotism (which includes pride and desire) rather than in love, tomorrow conquers. So does yesterday. The noise of the clock will overwhelm all stifling and will overcome all the fiddles that seek to drown its sound, for the fiddles depend upon time for the very possibility of rhythm and sequence. *Souviens-toi* is the noise of the clock and fittingly punctuates the poem.

We observe the rhythmical balance in the two lines quoted earlier. *Le jour décroît; la nuit augmente* establishes a regular accented rhythm. *Souviens-toi* balances as the completing one-third of the line. It benefits by resisting the rhythm of the first two clauses and asserting its own. This independence attracts notice. Coincidently it shifts time from the processes of nature, the rhythm of day and night, to the world of spirit and conscience. The next line continues the succession of clauses. *Le gouffre a toujours soif* is balanced against *la clepsydre se vide*. The past pours into abyss just as water pours from a water-clock, regularly and ineluctably. The gulf, or abyss, is the place where man attempts to rid himself of his manhood. It is where he both emulates the beast and imagines himself as a god-demon of ambition, pride, and cunning, of all manner of wickedness. The couplet is simple, yet very suggestive. Unusual for French poetry, its hexameter is stressed like English verse. This is effective for such a succession of clauses; it keeps them neatly partitioned while preserving the rhythmic tie between them.

Like much of Baudelaire's verse, "L'Horloge" contains shoddy work alongside the good. In several places not only are its expressions cliché, but also its technique is that of exhausted mediocrity.

Time sits on the city, devouring the instants of its prime of city pride, robbing it of glory in its wane, wasting the fresh muscle presented every instant. The heart sits within, sheltered by stones and timbers and chimney bricks. The heart lives on memories of love and peace. Outside the little room is mist, dirt, and the darkness with its lamps—that is, there is nothing outside the room but a dark expanse of wind and void. In this isolation, the heart secretes a bitter liquid and soaks in it without change of bath. This is its concentration on itself. It cannot go out to its fellows in unselfishness. It makes an inventory of shameful time past, present, and future. Such immersion in one's own fluids and exhaustion of the combinations and patterns of one's own personality was called *spleen* by Baudelaire. Every artery of escape has been seared shut. As the distillation is prolonged, the liquid becomes concentrated and heavy.

SPLEEN

Pluviôse, irrité contre la vie entière,
De son urne à grands flots verse un froid ténébreux
Aux pâles habitants du voisin cimetière
Et la mortalité sur les faubourgs brumeux.

Mon chat sur le carreau cherchant une litière
Agite sans repos son corps maigre et galeux;
L'âme d'un vieux poëte erre dans la gouttière
Avec la triste voix d'un fantôme frileux.

Le bourdon se lamente, et la bûche enfumée
Accompagne en fausset la pendule enrhumée,
Cependant qu'en un jeu plein de sales parfums,

Héritage fatal d'une vieille hydropique,
Le beau valet de cœur et la dame de pique
Causent sinistrement de leurs amours défunts.

SPLEEN

Rainy February, irritated against the whole of life,
Pours from his urn in great streams a dark coldness
On the pale inhabitants of the neighboring cemetery
And pours mortality on the foggy slums.

My cat seeking a litter on the floor
Agitates his lean and mangy body restlessly;
The soul of an old poet wanders in the gutter
With the sad voice of a chilly phantom.

The great bell mourns, and the smoking log
Accompanies in falsetto the rheumy clock,
Whilst in the filthy-smelling pack of cards,

Fatal inheritance of a fortune-telling crone,
The dandy Knave of Hearts and the Queen of Spades
Chat sinisterly of their defunct amours.

In this poem, irony has refined the suffering and shown it
in a double light. The problem is reduced and edited by

the rigorous selection of details for ironic effect. The weather, the cat, the gutter noise, the great bell, the burning log, and the clock are investigated. As if they were two more descriptive elements in this same series, the *valet de cœur* and the *dame de pique* are added casually, conversationally; and the poem is ended. The details have been collected to place the poet's feeling in an ironical perspective. The great skill and irony of technique is the masquerading of this feeling as if it were merely a final incident in the *décor*. In addition, the previous details have been purposely selected to anticipate this feeling.

The pressure of the metropolis outside is rendered in two strokes. First, the dead in the cemetery are showered with chill by the cold month Pluviôse, as if it were some celestial gift. Second, the *faubourgs* are showered with a similar gift, mortality, which is the wear and tear deposited by each city day of struggle for material welfare, and of endurance against misery. This wear and tear dissolves the fresh muscle produced by each day, and corrodes its regular diurnal share of life's barrier against death. Ironically, Pluviôse, the damp February of spleen, pours its chill of death and paralysis as if it were manna from a celestial cornucopia. Its lavishness falls to the splintery discolored skeletons stretched in the cold ground and to the deathly slums.

Now the poem turns from the general metropolitan scene to create its little room. A cat curves voluptuously in the warmth of this interior. It is sinuous without sound, so that there is no noise of living things in the scene. The whistle of the burning log and the wheeze of the clock represent the oppressive harmony of the heated interior. As in "L'Horloge," the clock marks the growth of the past in the continuous expiration of the present. The muffled slow clanging of a distant church bell and the wail of the wind, "the soul of an old poet," in the gutter come from the mysterious outer darkness. The suspense of this alternation of singular noises, coupled with the intricate curvilinear figures which the cat weaves upon the floor, creates an impression of fear. Cold skeletons, wind, and slums outside, and feline choreography, warmth, and counterpoint of sounds from inanimate objects inside, prepare us for some striking display of despair and suffering.

Baudelaire's masterful touch is that he utilizes this anticipation for ironic purposes. Apparently he merely throws in two more elements to complete the description of the scene. But when we look more closely at them, we see that they enact his state of mind, consummating the poem. A pack of cards lies spread out on the table before him. *Fatal*, they were fated to be his inheritance; they are cards which have come to him from a fortune-teller, who in this case is *the* Fortune Teller. Lying in the upturned cards is his effigy:

> *Le beau valet de cœur et la dame de pique*
> *Causent sinistrement de leurs amours défunts.*

> The dandy Knave of Hearts and the Queen of Spades
> Chat sinisterly of their defunct amours.

The Knave of Hearts and the Queen of Spades live in the pack of cards, and they are chattering. The pack of cards, perfumed with filth, has become Baudelaire's state of mind.

A fortune-teller would discern hints, clues, and outlines of destiny in the fatal pattern of the cards. The poem directs us simply to the Knave of Hearts and the Queen of Spades as the most representative signs. As a sign of Baudelaire's state of mind, the Knave of Hearts becomes the knave of the heart. He is the *beau valet de cœur, beau* being used to represent a bold perfection of manners and appearance in egotism. The Knave of Hearts typifies Baudelaire's *cœur* which at other times was equivalent in warmth and brilliance to the sun, and which now has shriveled up like that of Célimène. Equal to the Knave of Hearts and co-regnant with him is the Queen of Spades, who is also the queen of pique. This baleful card is the sign of spleen, sourness, and self-inspection of spirit. These two, red Prince and black

Queen, dominate the pack, equal and unchallenged in their power.

Knave and Queen have enacted Baudelaire's state of mind and completed the poem, not by a striking exhibition of despair, but ironically. *Causent* is the word which does the work, which concludes and at the same time composes the poem by sustaining the low tone of the previous stanzas. The conversation of the Knave and Queen which ends the poem demonstrates a state of mind which cannot rise to the occasion for despair because it does not have the strength to confront it in all its implications. Out of cowardice, the mind fumbles with dry memories and sentiments, devoting itself to a self-contained dialogue in order to distract itself from the terror of despair. In this state of mind, one cannot face the conditions of life and the despairing conditions of the evil which one has caused. Like the ostrich in his sand, one hides in the silly dialogues of *amours défunts.*

The second *Spleen* poem continues the scene laid down by the first, the same interior and exterior.

> *Un gros meuble à tiroirs encombré de bilans,*
> *De vers, de billets doux, de procès, de romances,*
> *Avec de lourds cheveux roulés dans des quittances,*
> *Cache moins de secrets que mon triste cerveau.*
> *C'est une pyramide, un immense caveau,*
> *Qui contient plus de morts que la fosse commune.*

> A big piece of furniture with drawers encumbered by
>   balance sheets,
> Verses, billets-doux, legal summons, ballads,
> With heavy locks of hair rolled up in receipts,
> Hides less secrets than my sorrowful brain.
> It is a pyramid, an immense vault,
> Which contains more dead than the common paupers'
>   grave.

J'ai plus de souvenirs que si j'avais mille ans. I have more memories than if I were a thousand years old, he says. This immense storage is insurance against despair. It is the material for many nights' contemplation. The collection in the chest of drawers which makes up his brain is heterogeneous and disorderly, so that its material can be recombined in an infinite number of patterns. Yet everything in it is dead. When the secrets, the solitary dialogues, and the memories give out, ennui alone remains:

> Rien n'égale en longueur les boiteuses journées,
> Quand sous les lourds flocons des neigeuses années
> L'ennui, fruit de la morne incuriosité,
> Prend les proportions de l'immortalité.

> Nothing equals in length the limping days
> When, under the heavy flakes of snowy years,
> Ennui, the fruit of sad incuriosity,
> Assumes the proportions of immortality.

Winter, since it locks the poet alone in small rooms and makes the exterior world even less real, is the season symbolic of ennui. In ennui, time is observed very differently because movement and change seem meaningless. It takes the proportions of immortality which is considered to be timeless under the Platonic assumptions. Yet it does not succeed, because time is observed by its very slowness of progression. In ennui, we wait anxiously for time to pass. In the Platonic conception of immortality, no time is remarked, since it is merely one of the limits of the world of appearances.

The third *Spleen* poem, dealing with the impotence of distractions to revive the victim of ennui, has been discussed on page 41.

The fourth *Spleen* poem develops from its three predecessors. Its first three stanzas are in a low tone of melancholy, each beginning with *Quand* and describing, first, the heavy sky weighing like a lid on our spirits; second, the resemblance of Hope to a bat's wings beating the walls of a dungeon; and third, the vast prison of the rain in which spiders weave their webs around our brains. The fourth stanza brings a sudden shift in tone, which has a startling effect against the melancholy, polysyllabic meters of the preceding stanzas:

Des cloches tout à coup sautent avec furie . . .

Bells suddenly explode in fury . . .

Consonants prevail, and the rhythm is sharp and severe, far from the smooth flow of the preceding stanzas. This contrast enhances the shock of the bell-ringing line as much as it is possible for musical effects in poetry to do so. The fifth and concluding stanza is anticlimactic and relapses to the melancholy tone of the first three after the eruption in the fourth stanza.

SPLEEN

Quand le ciel bas et lourd pèse comme un couvercle
Sur l'esprit gémissant en proie aux longs ennuis,
Et que de l'horizon embrassant tout le cercle
Il nous verse un jour noir plus triste que les nuits;

Quand la terre est changée en un cachot humide,
Où l'Espérance, comme une chauve-souris,
S'en va battant les murs de son aile timide
Et se cognant la tête à des plafonds pourris;

Quand la pluie étalant ses immenses traînées
D'une vaste prison imite les barreaux,
Et qu'un peuple muet d'infâmes araignées
Vient tendre ses filets au fond de nos cerveaux,

Des cloches tout à coup sautent avec furie
Et lancent vers le ciel un affreux hurlement,
Ainsi que des esprits errants et sans patrie
Qui se mettent à geindre opiniâtrément.

—Et de longs corbillards, sans tambours ni musique,
Défilent lentement dans mon âme; l'Espoir,

Vaincu, pleure, et l'Angoisse atroce, despotique,
Sur mon crâne incliné plante son drapeau noir.

SPLEEN

When the heavy and low sky weighs like a lid
On the groaning spirit prey to long ennuis,
And when, embracing the entire circle of the horizon,
A black day sadder than the nights is poured upon us;

When the earth is changed into a humid dungeon,
Where Hope, like a bat,
Goes striking the walls with his timid wing
And bumping his head against rotted ceilings;

When the rain, spreading out his immense trails,
Imitates the bars of a vast prison,
And when a mute throng of infamous spiders
Come to stretch their nets at the back of our brains,

Bells suddenly explode in fury
And fling a frightful howling towards the sky,
Like wandering spirits without country
Who set themselves at moaning obstinately.

—And long funeral processions, without drums or music,
March past slowly in my soul; Hope,
Conquered, weeps, and atrocious anguish, despotic,
Plants his black flag on my inclined skull.

The sky as a lid and the earth as a dungeon in the first two
stanzas continue the locale of the preceding three poems:
the small room, the ennuis, the fog and gloom outside in
metropolis, and the despair of the victim. The next stanza
bridges the gap between the internal world of the victim's
state of mind and the external world through which communication must be made. The prison of the rain and the
spider webs around the brain are the nexus between the
poet and the external world. An identity is established;

each of them, poet and world, assumes the other into itself. Rain-prison and spider web are the closest correspondents of his state of mind that can be found in the physical world. To us, they are the victim. They are qualitatively the utmost which can be communicated about him. Notice that no abstract statement of feeling is made. Two images are shown in lieu of that statement which is the technique of communication in inferior verse.

The atmosphere has been forced with suspense. The explosion of the bells in stanza four is the sudden storm toward which the poem has been cumulating its thunderhead. The explosion is the outburst of spleen, raging violently to ease the tension and suspense of intolerable despair, then subsiding. The bells, driving in upon his melancholy, open up the ground around him in every direction by revealing the relationship which his state of mind has with the fundaments of life: "In certain almost supernatural states of mind, the profundity of life reveals itself whole in the spectacle, ordinary as it seems, which is under one's eyes. The spectacle becomes the symbol of this profundity."

The profundity of life is revealed not by visual spectacle, but by the explosion of the bells in this poem. The noise breaks in upon the melancholy and demonstrates the layers of significance implied by his state of mind which had previously been playing listlessly over the surface of these layers. The bells make a sudden vertical penetration in depth. This draws the whole into flawless concentration, like the sudden formation of a faceted crystal. The single line which explodes the bells *avec furie* precipitates the crystal out of its solution. To use another metaphor, this line is the treebole for whose eruption above the soil the other parts of the poem as roots provide sustenance. Through it we see wholly.

The bells act in sympathy with the victim's despair. They release it in an ecstasy of enormous volume. By actuating the bells, the despair becomes a triumph and a cry of warlike pagan pride. Despair is carried to Valhalla and glorified when the bells explode. Despair and spleen have become intolerable and demand in their pride to possess the world as a means of exhausting the repressed anguish of their nerves. Paradoxically, in his spleen the sufferer is both victim of the world, containing himself as it does, and conqueror viking of the world which is only an appearance beside his furious pride: *Des cloches tout à coup sautent avec furie.* This is the essence of spleen; it is pride masquerading as despair. It shifts erratically from exultation and self-intoxication to fits of depression, ennui, and disgust. *Le beau valet de cœur et la dame du pique* chatter on; the heavy flakes of ennui fall in *neigeuses années*; the rain becomes a prison and spiders twist their nets tight around the lobes of the brain. And startlingly from the midst of this mass of gray mist, damp *faubourgs*, and crabbed self-pity, a geyser of pride spouts dazzlingly, impelled by the volcanic and subterranean engines of sulphurous egotism. *Des cloches tout à coup sautent avec furie.* This is spleen.

We have examined the mind of the victim of sin and metropolitan civilization in his little room where the metropolis is merely implicit outside. We can now move out into the city and bring the background close enough within view to pick out well-defined details. The background becomes explicit. Here is the landscape as presented in the first of the *Tableaux Parisiens*, Baudelaire's city-scenes.

Je veux, pour composer chastement mes églogues,
Coucher auprès du ciel, comme les astrologues,
Et, voisin des clochers, écouter en rêvant
Leurs hymnes solennels emportés par le vent.
Les deux mains au menton, du haut de ma mansarde,
Je verrai l'atelier qui chante et qui bavarde;
Les tuyaux, les clochers, ces mâts de la cité,
Et les grands ciels qui font rêver d'éternité.

Il est doux, à travers les brumes, de voir naître
L'étoile dans l'azur, la lampe à la fenêtre,
Les fleuves de charbon monter au firmament. . . .

To compose chastely my eclogues, I wish
To couch close to the sky, like the astrologers,
And, neighbor to the steeples, to listen while dreaming
To their solemn hymns which are carried away by the
    wind.
My two hands at my chin, from the height of my garret,
I shall see the great workshop which sings and chatters;
The chimney flues, the steeples, these masts of the city,
And the great skies which make me dream of eternity.

> It is pleasing to see through the fogs the star
> Arising in the azure, the lamp at the window,
> The great rivers of coal mounting to the firmament. . . .

Baudelaire lies close above the city watching many phases of
its activity simultaneously from his vantage point. He is
perched on the topmost rigging in this mastyard of resonant
steeples and dirty chimney pipes. From these flues, separate
parallel channels of gassy smoke unite to form not rivers
but great tidal estuaries which ascend interminably into
the ocean of the sky. The vertiginous firmament is clear and
bitter as salt, intoxicating the nostrils and brow. This great
air twinges, and swells in and out, vibrating from the clangor
of the bells.

We should remember that Baudelaire provides his initial
landscape of the city in the form of a *volupté*. *Volupté* is
in this particular case arrived at through intoxication with
the rhythm of continuous sound combined with the immense vista of the sky. He concludes the poem:

> Car je serai plongé dans cette volupté
> D'évoquer le Printemps avec ma volonté,
> De tirer un soleil de mon cœur, et de faire
> De mes pensers brûlants une tiède atmosphère.

> For I shall be plunged in this voluptuousness
> Of evoking Springtime with my will,
> Of drawing a sun from my heart and of making
> A mild atmosphere from my burning thoughts.

In his garret during the cold season, he creates a vision of
volupté and thus discovers spring in the winter. Signifi-
cantly, his aim is *De tirer un soleil de mon cœur*—to draw
a sun from my heart. In these city-scenes where swans and
old women wander piteously, the heart is released from
its nadir of hibernation when it was the frozen red cube of
"Chant d'Automne," and is reinstated in its incandescent
zenith as a sun of sympathy and unselfish love. By its own

sun-heat, the heart wittily contrives to change the cold of winter into the mild atmosphere of spring. Having established his landscape and having placed his heart in the center of it to provide a sun of illumination, Baudelaire examines the particulars of the city.

Andromaque, *je pense à vous!*—here is the swan escaped from its menagerie into this city,

> ce camp de baraques,
> Ces tas de chapiteaux ébauchés et de fûts,
> Les herbes, les gros blocs verdis par l'eau des flaques,

> this camp of sheds,
> This heap of roughed-out capitals and shafts,
> The grasses, the large stone blocks made green by the
> water of the puddles.

I saw in early morning

> à l'heure où sous les cieux
> Froids et clairs le Travail s'éveille, où la voirie
> Pousse un sombre ouragan dans l'air silencieux,

> Un cygne qui s'était évadé de sa cage,
> Et de ses pieds palmés frottant le pavé sec,
> Sur le sol raboteux traînait son grand plumage.
> Près d'un ruisseau sans eau la bête ouvrant le bec,

> Baignait nerveusement ses ailes dans la poudre,
> Et disait, le cœur plein de son beau lac natal:
> "Eau, quand donc pleuvras-tu? quand tonneras-tu, fou-
> dre?"

> at the hour when work
> Awakens under cold and clear skies, when the sewer
> Pushes a gloomy hurricane into the silent air,

> A swan which had escaped from his cage,
> Rubbing the dry pavement with his webbed feet,
> Dragged his grand plumage on the rough ground.
> Opening his beak beside a dry gutter,

He bathed his wings nervously in the dust,
And, heart full of his happy natal lake, said:
"Water, when then will you rain down? When will you
   strike, thunderbolt?"

Only at the dawn hour just before the laborers awaken does
the city appear completely inanimate. Ghostly, deserted,
there is not a movement; and along the endless reaches of
stone buildings and stone streets stretching to every point of
the horizon there is not a sound, except for the suppressed
tumult of the sewer. The city-scene is purposely deserted
to present the swan in his full symbolic value. The beautiful
and immaculate bird wanders clumsily among an empty in-
terminable waste of noiseless stone masses, pavements, and
inscrutable blocks of buildings whose countless eyes are extinct. There is no water left in this arid stone. There everything is inanimate and water is unnecessary. The lost bird,
stray animate, ruffles its feathers in the powdery dust of a
dry gutter, performing the ritual of living things. But the
nourishing refreshment given to flesh and blood when it
engages in its ceremonious bath is lacking.

Eau, quand donc pleuvras-tu? Quand tonneras-tu, foudre?

Water, when then will you rain down? When will you
  'strike, thunderbolt?

When will lightning crack open the massy core of stone
so that vivifying rain can pierce its flinted heart and bring
forth verdure in the desert? We realize that the swan is the
emblem of man alone among the abstractions and inanimate objects to which his fellows have given their devotion.
Preoccupied with the arrangement of their physical cosmos,
they are dead in life, inanimates caught in a rigorous chain
of cause and effect which determines them to erect their
graceless polylithic structures. Represented as a swan, the
man who seeks life finds no water in their desert. Life must
come in the form of rain and thunder, bringing with it the

wisdom of the fruitful expense of the self. Baudelaire's swan presents the same theme developed by T. S. Eliot's Death by Water motif and presented in "What the Thunder Said." The rain and thunder message of "give, sympathize, and control" resolves this concluding section of the principal work of Eliot's earlier period, the baroque *Waste Land*.

> . . . *palais neufs, échafaudages, blocs,*
> *Vieux faubourgs, tout pour moi devient allégorie.* . . .

> *Je pense à mon grand cygne, avec ses gestes fous,*
> *Comme les exilés, ridicule et sublime,*
> *Et rongé d'un désir sans trêve! et puis à vous,*

> *Andromaque, des bras d'un grand époux tombée,*
> *Vil bétail, sous la main du superbe Pyrrhus,*
> *Auprès d'un tombeau vide en extase courbée;*
> *Veuve d'Hector, hélas! et femme d'Hélénus!*[1]

> *Je pense à la négresse, amaigrie et phtisique,*
> *Piétinant dans la boue, et cherchant, l'œil hagard,*
> *Les cocotiers absents de la superbe Afrique*
> *Derrière la muraille immense du brouillard.*

> . . . *new palaces, scaffoldings, blocks,*
> *Old quarters of the city, all becomes allegory for me.* . . .

> *I think of my great swan, with his mad gestures,*
> *Ridiculous and sublime, like the exiled,*
> *And gnawed by a truceless desire! and then I think of you,*

> *Andromache, fallen from the arms of a great husband,*
> *A low chattel, under the hand of superb Pyrrhus,*
> *Bent in ecstasy beside an empty tomb;*
> *Widow of Hector, alas! and wife of Helenus.*

> *I think of the negress, emaciated and consumptive,*
> *Stamping in the mud, and seeking with haggard glance*

[1] Eliot himself has justly pointed out the Racinian style, syntax, and rhythm of this stanza.

The absent coconut palms of superb Africa
Behind the immense walling of the fog.

The allegory performed before the city-scene is that of exile: Andromache, the hero's consort, is a captured slave. Andromache, the swan, and the negress have been deprived of their birthright. The ecstasy of heroic gesture—ecstasy even beside the tomb—the refreshing beauty of the living bird, and the fleshly rhythm of untamed continents are sold in the city. The trade is made in exhausting and brutalizing pleasure, and in food and shelter. The birthright is sold for bread, but the bread turns to stone in the victim's hands. The victim asks for bread and the city hands him a stone. Now the swan and the negress chew on stone and are crazed by the juice of stone, as stricken mariners are crazed by drinking salt water. The negress has bartered and lost forever the suppleness of her savage body; the swan wallows in filth; Andromache, widow of Hector, is the slave and concubine of a proud conqueror.

This sale is an allegory, and the city, as Baudelaire said, is an allegorical background. The auction is not the result of metropolis as a specific scene. But metropolis is a convenient image of the modern false community. The purpose of this community is the accumulation of commodities through the division of labor, or through fraud and usury. Heroism, beauty, and instinctive savage grace, represented by Andromache, the swan, and the negress, become commodities for exchange and thus are sterile qualities. Similarly, spirit and flesh are exchanged for commodities, for the stupefaction of pleasure, and for the exhilaration of egotism. The evil is not to be blamed on metropolis; the large city is merely the most compelling allegorical vehicle, since it is the usual background for such barter.

"Les Petites Vieilles" exhibits a set of victims who extend the series of Andromache, swan, and negress. These are the little old women tottering about the city. Like mummies

dragged about at Egyptian feasts, they mirror back the
skeleton to all flesh which passes in the prime of its vanity
before them.

Dans les plis sinueux des vieilles capitales, . . .

Ils rampent, flagellés par les bises iniques,
Frémissant au fracas roulant des omnibus,
Et serrant sur leur flanc, ainsi que des reliques,
Un petit sac brodé de fleurs ou de rébus;

Ils trottent, tout pareils à des marionnettes;
Se traînent, comme font les animaux blessés,
Ou dansent, sans vouloir danser, pauvres sonnettes.

Vous qui fûtes la grâce ou qui fûtes la gloire,
Nul ne vous reconnaît! un ivrogne incivil
Vous insulte en passant d'un amour dérisoire;
Sur vos talons gambade un enfant lâche et vil.

Où serez-vous demain, Eves octogénaires,
Sur qui pèse la griffe effroyable de Dieu?

In the sinuous folds of ancient capitals, . . .

They creep, scourged by the iniquitous north winds,
Trembling at the rolling tumult of the omnibus,
And pressing on their hip, like relics,
A little bag embroidered with flowers or rebus;

They trot, exactly like marionettes;
Drag themselves along, as wounded animals do,
Or dance without wanting to dance, poor metal bells.

You who were grace, or who were glory,
No one recognizes you! A rude drunkard
Passing by insults you with a derisive proposal of passion;
A vile and cowardly urchin gambols at your heels.

Where will you be tomorrow, octogenarian Eves,
On whom the frightful claw of God lies heavy?

Brittle and rigid, dry as fallen leaves, these creatures are blown through the city. The wind is the sign of their helplessness and will-lessness. They are wholly within its caprice; they flutter like marionettes wherever the wind wills. The shape of their skirts invites us to compare the old ladies to bells. This is fortunate, because we can proceed to have them shiver, rattle, and swing spasmodically, as if they were jangled by an arbitrary bell-puller. The brutality of the wind and the fragility of the victims excite our pity. The most piteous image lies in their resemblance to wounded animals, as they drag along *dans les plis sinueux de vieilles capitales*—in the sinuous folds of ancient capitals. Likewise, in his *Petits Poèmes en Prose*, Baudelaire describes a similar set of pets who had once been nourished and loved but were later driven out into the city: "The calamitous dogs who wander, solitary, in the sinuous ravines of immense capitals. 'Where do the dogs go?'"

Baudelaire extends the heart of sympathy to these wounded, to mothers wronged by their children, mothers whose sons have been killed, wives abused by their husbands. These events happened long ago; the women have been wandering since then. But the decrepit courtesans and queens show his principal allegory. These are the masks of decay that pass through the city, executing a *danse macabre* before the folly of the living. The sinners are the resource of this rambling poem: as Eves, they continue to expiate their sins in old age.

When the moon rises above the city, it observes the usual romantic scenes—Endymion, lovers, poets seeking the Muse, and the conventionally horrible sight of vipers copulating by moonlight. But this is byplay to set up the genuine horror of spiritual desolation which is embodied in the woman of the concluding tercet.

LA LUNE OFFENSÉE

O Lune qu'adoraient discrètement nos pères,
Du haut des pays bleus où, radieux sérail,
Les astres vont te suivre en pimpant attirail,
Ma vieille Cynthia, lampe de nos repaires,

Vois-tu les amoureux sur leurs grabats prospères,
De leur bouche en dormant montrer le frais émail?
Le poëte buter du front sur son travail?
Ou sous les gazons secs s'accoupler les vipères?

Sous ton domino jaune, et d'un pied clandestin,
Vas-tu, comme jadis, du soir jusqu'au matin,
Baiser d'Endymion les grâces surannées?

—"Je vois ta mère, enfant de ce siècle appauvri,
Qui vers son miroir penche un lourd amas d'années,
Et plâtre artistement le sein qui t'a nourri!"

THE OFFENDED MOON

O Moon, whom our fathers adored discreetly,
From the height of the blue countries where, radiant
  seraglio,
The stars go following you in smart finery,
My good old Cynthia, lamp of our familiar haunts,

Do you see the lovers on their prosperous pallets,
Showing as they sleep the fresh enamel of their mouth,
The poet propping his brow above his work,
Or the vipers coupling deep in the dry turf?

Beneath your yellow domino, and on clandestine feet,
Are you going, as formerly, to kiss from evening until
  morn
The outmoded charms of Endymion?

—"I see your mother, child of this impoverished century,
Who leans toward her mirror a heavy mass of years,

And paints and whitens artistically the bosom which
    nourished you."

The delicate conceit of the seraglio of stars fittingly com-
pliments *Ma vieille Cynthia*, playfully and affectionately
named. It is Laforgue's moon without any doubt: *lampe de
nos repaires*, providing friendly and convenient illumination wherever caprice could lead the fantastics. Like the
masked harlequins and pierrots of Laforgue's midnight, the
moon wears Laforgue's domino, and steps *d'un pied clandestin*—on clandestine feet—to kiss Endymion, another
masquer, though out of date like all the conventional tableaux described in the poem. This has all been delightful
and witty: the moon and Pierrot, even the nasty snakes
writhing in the moonlight. Upon this nocturne is forced a
concluding scene of corrupt, weary, and vulgar display: the
mother *Qui vers son miroir penche un lourd amas d'années*—who leans toward her mirror a heavy mass of years.
She is hideous; she is heavy; she covers her dead breast with
powder; she wishes to join the *danse macabre* and swing on
the trapeze of lust, though her powdered painted limbs are
swollen and difficult to move.

And in Laforgue's Paris, as the night waxes,

On entend çà et là les cuisines siffler,
Les théâtres glapir, les orchestres ronfler.

Here and there one hears the kitchens whistling,
The theatres yelping, the orchestras rumbling and snort-
    ing.

Siffler, glapir, ronfler—these are Laforgue's verbs appearing long before him in Baudelaire's city. Laforgue's Paris
is but a part of Baudelaire's

Fourmillante cité, cité pleine de rêves,
Où le spectre en plein jour raccroche le passant!

Swarming city, city full of dreams,
Where in broad daylight the specter lays hold of the
    passer-by!

{ 109 }

It is different from Eliot's Unreal City; it is full of noise and concupiscent movement; doors open and shut, giving the dark street bright white glimpses of carousal, gaming and whoring in countless cabarets. Everything opens up as the night advances:

> La Prostitution s'allume dans les rues;
> Comme une fourmilière elle ouvre ses issues.

> Prostitution lights up in the streets;
> Like an ant-hill she opens her issuances.

Compounded atop this burgeoning of black night and brilliant light from interiors, and straying in and out among this noise and debauchery, are the heart's piteous figures— Andromache, the swan, the negress, the old women. These are the specters of the fourmillante cité that, grafted into its outrageous lust, grow and grow as immense confused symbols, shimmering in and out among the background of city night and day. They expand beyond the mind's power of assimilation:

> Vainement ma raison voulait prendre la barre;
> La tempête en jouant déroutait ses efforts,
> Et mon âme dansait, dansait, vieille gabarre
> Sans mâts, sur une mer monstrueuse et sans bords!

> Vainly my reason wished to take the helm;
> The tempest, playing about, led its efforts astray,
> And my soul was dancing, dancing, old lighter
> Without masts, on a monstrous and limitless sea.

9

We remember that the city scene opened with the desire *de tirer un soleil de mon cœur*—to draw a sun from my heart. The heart through its sympathy brings to life the particulars that symbolize the nature of the city. The sun is equivalent to the heart; it is he who in the city

> *commande aux moissons de croître et de mûrir*
> *Dans le cœur immortel qui toujours veut fleurir.* . . .

> *Et s'introduit en roi, sans bruit et sans valets,*
> *Dans tous les hôpitaux et dans tous les palais.*

> commands harvests to grow and ripen
> In the immortal heart which wishes always to blossom. . . .

> And introduces himself as a king, without ostentation
>   and without footmen,
> In all the hospitals and in all the palaces.

In the city, the sun strengthens the heart and symbolizes its diffusion of sympathy. Especially at dawn or sunset, the sun hangs in the breast in place of the heart, suffusing the balcony scene with peace and calm joy, and supporting the heart in all its associations.

> *Que le Soleil est beau quand tout frais il se lève,*
> *Comme une explosion nous lançant son bonjour!*

> How beautiful is the sun when he arises, all fresh,
> Casting at us, like an explosion, his bonjour!

This is the sun of joy. It courses above the earth all day and expires brilliantly in the Romantic sunset: *Le Coucher du*

{ 111 }

Soleil Romantique. It escapes irreparably; it cannot be caught; its promise cannot be actualized.

> —*Courons vers l'horizon, il est tard, courons vite,*
> *Pour attraper au moins un oblique rayon!*

> —*Let us run toward the horizon, it is late, run quickly,*
> *To catch at least an oblique beam.*

Romantically, the gold is beyond the horizon. Ironically, nothing remains in the twilight except *des crapauds imprévus et de froids limaçons*—unforeseen toads, cold snails. Yet the sun comes to assume the function of providing actual peace. It arouses emotive feeling and combines it with a liberation of the mind from present anguish. The result is a state of *cœur*.

> *Je n'ai pas oublié, voisine de la ville,*
> *Notre blanche maison, petite mais tranquille;*
> *Sa Pomone de plâtre et sa vieille Vénus*
> *Dans un bosquet chétif cachant leurs membres nus,*
> *Et le soleil, le soir, ruisselant et superbe,*
> *Qui, derrière la vitre où se brisait sa gerbe,*
> *Semblait, grand œil ouvert dans le ciel curieux,*
> *Contempler nos dîners longs et silencieux,*
> *Répandant largement ses beaux reflets de cierge*
> *Sur la nappe frugale et les rideaux de serge.*

> *I have not forgotten our house close to the city,*
> *Our white house, small but tranquil;*
> *Its plaster Pomona and its old Venus*
> *Hiding their bare limbs in its sparse shrubbery,*
> *And the sun, at evening, streaming and superb,*
> *Who, behind the windowglass where he dashed his sheaf*
> *   of beams,*
> *Seemed, great open eye in the inquisitive sky,*
> *To contemplate our long and silent dinners,*

Spreading largely his fine candle flashes
On the frugal tablecloth and the curtains of serge.

Biographically, this is Baudelaire's mother's Neuilly home
which the child viewed as the background of happiness. The
idea of *volupté* enters into the poem—the idea of serenity
and harmony. The house, the statues, are fitting. The sunset extends the harmony to make it universal in the exterior
scene. The light is cool, the serene clarity of the light of
volupté, not thc lustful heat of noon. *Ruisselant* actualizes
this, suggesting long drippings of light, cool, translucent,
and distant. The sun, an "open eye" at sunset, when we can
easily look directly at him, brings the room to life and makes
of it a jewel, even to the serge curtains and the frugal napery.
The dinner is long and silent, suggesting stately movement
and gesture, without sound or color. Those who contemplate the sun from an immense distance move within the
dining room as if in a trance.

The poem floats; it is purely descriptive; an exterior followed by an interior; and yet it renders the trance of contemplation, the dullness of the senses, the daze in which
we are sometimes captured and stilled, when we are without thought. The poem presents this by the splendid illumination of the dining room which makes a tableau of the
motions of the diners. Their motions become ritual; *longs
et silencieux* they move ceremonially, bathed in the sunset
which commands their senses. The exterior scene is likewise
a tableau, with its plaster statues formally placed in the
small garden about the doll's house. The tone of this still
composition enters into the interior; the entire scene is
paralyzed in contemplation. The presence of the actual con-
templators is indicated only in the line about *nos dîners*.
The magical fascination of the sun is sustained by the use
of *cierge—reflets de cierge*. The flash and fire of the sun
becomes diluted at sunset to the strength of candles, but

the candles are myriad; the room is full of cool white light of low intensity.

The feeling of *volupté* has been aroused. It is rooted in harmony and correspondence. The universe sways in cadence, or is held tranced in contemplation. There are no loose ends. Dullness of some of the senses has diminished the individuality of the practical, bourgeois man. But in the decadence of the old senses new ones thrive, and the individuality of dream becomes pronounced as the practical individuality is relaxed. Philosophically, there are obvious indications of pantheism in *volupté*. But the individuality is released, not swallowed up. The senses are dazed and expanded immeasurably. Each individuality assumes the universe as its reflection and expression; the universe does not assume the individuality into itself. The universal seas sway with the vessel they support; the movement is all ritual.

This *volupté*, this expansion of the self, this fascination with universal rhythm is pagan philosophy, old stuff to be sure, but firmly grounded in the experience of many sensitive persons. Not that we must seek out a quorum to justify it. We merely indicate the persistence of this idea, or psychology, a psychology akin to Proust's in its victories over time and space. We can now confront this *volupté* of Baudelaire with his Christian aspirations. As a Christian, Baudelaire vacillated, squirmed, and wriggled. Although we view his mature years as a Pilgrim's Progress through the exhausting fires of sin, we must admit that his beliefs are difficult to track down. Let us consider that his Christian beliefs do not forbid his experiences of *volupté*. When he is expositing or undergoing *volupté*, he is not worshiping nature, or searching for a religion in it. Neither is he worshiping his personal Lord. *Volupté* should not be considered as a religious experience. It is an experience of the harmony between man and the scene in which he finds himself. Both man and the landscapes with which he is surrounded are the handiwork of the Creator. The recognition of the harmony and common origin of the man and his landscape is the experience of *volupté*, of fascinated ecstasy and daze. It is pure pleasure, and yet not pride. This recognition is not religious; it does not seek rapport with the Creator. It does however acknowledge the harmony and complementary nature of His landscapes and His creatures.

For Baudelaire, as for many of us, there is no such thing as a natural world or cosmos in the Aristotelian sense. The concept of the natural world as a measurable entity, the concepts of cosmology and cosmogony, are meaningless. The natural world is merely a succession of landscapes traversed by the spirit. It is a *mise en scène*, like the garden of Eden, for the drama of the soul. These landscapes are collections of qualities and symbols; as landscapes they cannot be quantified or solidified. The landscapes are appearances without substance and as such continually reforming and realigning their patterns as the spirit traverses them. This Platonic viewpoint is congenital; it cannot comprehend such an abstraction as the definitive Aristotelian cosmos of quantity, agency, and measure, which is the modern cosmos. The Aristotelian natural world has no apprehensible existence. For the Platonist, there are only landscapes.

When Baudelaire comes across a landscape whose qualities and symbols are harmonious with those of his spirit, he experiences this *volupté*, or communion. In the poem last quoted, the magnificence of the sun's visitation brings peace and the clemency of harmony.

Et le soleil le soir, ruisselant et superbe.

And the sun, at evening, streaming and superb.

Beauty, order, and superabundance of rhythm; *luxe, calme et volupté*—these are Flowers of Evil only in the sense that they have been forced up through a soil of lust and egotism. Baudelaire has clean flowers, but he calls them black *pour épater le bourgeois*, to make a sensation.

Volupté is composed of three images and one rhythm. Woman, ship, and cat are the images. As hair links woman with cat, sails link ship with woman, through her gowns. And all three images of volupté depend on the sea for their movement, as the ship does. The cat's eyes are made of metal and agate, clairs fanaux, vivantes opales, étoilés de parcelles d'or, qui me contemplent fixement—clear lamps, living opals, starred with particles of gold, which contemplate me steadily. In their movements, their electric bodies are puissants et doux, powerful and smoothly easy of movement.

The naked woman wearing only her jewels delights him with Ce monde rayonnant de métal et de pierre—this world radiant with metal and stone. Like a cat, she paces around him noiseless except for the clinking of her jewels:

> Et son bras et sa jambe, et sa cuisse et ses reins,
> Polis comme de l'huile, onduleux comme un cygne,
> Passaient devant mes yeux clairvoyants et sereins;
> Et son ventre et ses seins, ces grappes de ma vigne . . .

> And her arm and her leg, her thigh and her loins,
> Polished as if of oil, undulating as a swan,
> Passed before my clairvoyant and serene eyes;
> And her belly and her breasts, those clusters on my vine . . .

In her hair:

> La langoureuse Asie et la brûlante Afrique,
> Tout un monde lointain, absent, presque défunt,
> Vit dans tes profondeurs, forêt aromatique!
> Fortes tresses, soyez la houle qui m'enlève!
> Tu contiens, mer d'ébène, un éblouissant rêve
> De voiles, de rameurs, de flammes et de mâts,
> Où les vaisseaux glissant dans l'or et dans la moire, . . .
> Je plongerai ma tête amoureuse d'ivresse
> Dans ce noir océan où l'autre est enfermé;
> Et mon esprit subtil que le roulis caresse

Saura vous retrouver, ô féconde paresse,
Infinis bercements du loisir embaumé!

Languorous Asia and burning Africa,
An entire world, distant, absent, almost defunct,
Lives in your depths, aromatic forest!
Strong tresses, be the billow which carries me away!
Sea of ebony, you contain a dazzling dream
Of sails, of oarsmen, of pendants and of masts,
Where vessels sliding in gold and moire, . . .
I will plunge my head, enamoured of intoxication,
Into this dark ocean in which the other ocean is enclosed;
And my subtle spirit which the sea-rolling caresses
Will know how to find you again, O fecund idleness,
Infinite rockings of balmy leisure!

The dark hair, undulating like a cat's hide, contains a sea
which is continually rocking. The hair, like the cat, sways
and rolls to this rhythm of the swell of the sea. The hair,
flowing out, describes leisurely, stately curves. As Baudelaire
says elsewhere: "In the caresses of your head of hair, I find
again the languors of long hours passed on a divan in the
cabin of a fine ship, rocked by the imperceptible rolling of
the harbor water." The movements of the woman are as
easy, graceful, and effortless as those caused by the sea. The
woman is a ship, "Le Beau Navire":

Quand tu vas balayant l'air de ta jupe large,
Tu fais l'effet d'un beau vaisseau qui prend le large,
        Chargé de toile, et va roulant
Suivant un rythme doux, et paresseux, et lent.

Sur ton cou large et rond, sur tes épaules grasses,
Ta tête se pavane avec d'étranges grâces;
        D'un air placide et triomphant
Tu passes ton chemin, majestueuse enfant.

When you go sweeping the air with your full skirt,
You look like a fine ship which stands out to sea,
        Laden with sail, and goes rolling
Following a rhythm easy, indolent, and slow.

On your large round neck, on your plump shoulders,
Your head proceeds with unfamiliar graces;
        With a placid and triumphant air
You pass along your way, majestic child.

The skirts are sails; the head is a mast, swaying proudly.
    The perfection of *volupté* is rendered in the next poem
which combines the images of cat, ship, and woman, and
involves them in the triumph of ease: marine movement.
The woman's eyes are the cat's mineral eyes; her skirts are
the ship's sails; her movements are the luxurious shifts of
mode and pattern which are the movements of the sea-
swell; her tall masts ride the crests and pitch majestically
up and down in the sea-hollows:

Avec ses vêtements ondoyants et nacrés,
Même quand elle marche on croirait qu'elle danse,
Comme ces longs serpents que les jongleurs sacrés
Au bout de leurs bâtons agitent en cadence.

Comme le sable morne et l'azur des déserts,
Insensibles tous deux à l'humaine souffrance,
Comme les longs réseaux de la houle des mers,
Elle se développe avec indifférence.

Ses yeux polis sont faits de minéraux charmants,
Et dans cette nature étrange et symbolique
Où l'ange inviolé se mêle au sphinx antique,

Où tout n'est qu'or, acier, lumière et diamants,
Resplendit à jamais, comme un astre inutile,
La froide majesté de la femme stérile.

With her undulating and pearly vestments
Even when she walks one would believe that she is danc-
ing,
Like the long serpents which the sacred jugglers
Shake in cadence at the end of their staffs.

Like the gloomy sand and azure of the deserts,
Both insensible to human suffering,
Like the long networks of the sea-billows,
She develops with indifference.

Her polished eyes are made of charming minerals,
And in this strange and symbolic nature
Where the inviolate angel mixes with the antique sphinx,

Where all is but gold, steel, light and diamonds,
There is resplendent forever, like a useless star,
The cold majesty of the sterile woman.

The woman evoked is immense and symbolic, moving
in cadence, swaying hugely on the horizon. She is the spirit
of harmony and the serene madonna of cool rapport and
volupté in all the choiring reverberations of an attuned cosmos, a forest of symbols in perfect relationship. She depends
on the sea for her strength, as Antaeus drew life from his
earth-mother. She is incantation and genius of the sea,
swaying in it and above it and entering into the poem
through the sea which is her symbol, the most sensible of
her manifestations. She, like the sea, "offers both the idea
of immensity and of movement. Six or seven leagues of sea
represent for man a ray or a beam of the infinite. Behold a
diminutive infinite." By means of the sea, the woman, and
the ship, and the rhythm of their undulous orbiting, a
volupté is aroused which entrances the spirit away from the
world of strife and becoming to that of eternal forms and
complete harmony:
"I believe that the infinite and mysterious charm which
lies in the contemplation of a ship, and especially of a ship

in movement, partakes, in the first place, of regularity and symmetry, which are primary needs of the human spirit, to the same degree as complication and harmony; and in the second place this charm partakes of the successive multiplication and generation of all the curves and imaginary figures worked in space by the real elements of the object."

"The poetic idea which disengages itself from this working of movement in lines is the hypothesis of a being spacious, immense, complicated, but eurhythmic an animal full of genius."

The woman of the poem is such a being, except that she has no relation to human suffering and human ambition. When she walks, she dances, scattering those brilliant curves and collections of lines generated by her figure as she undulates through space. She leaves behind her a succession of line-sketches, each depicting the relation of her form to space at an instant of her movement. She is made to progress without motion of limb, like a moon or a star. She is made to reflect light cunningly and to clothe herself in it coolly. Silvery disk, she is majestic. *Astre inutile*, she turns about the earth, craning all necks, chilling all eyes. *Femme stérile*, there is no blood on her loins. Lustrous and entrancing she, like Botticelli's Venus and Madonna, is not made of flesh, but of gold, steel, light, and diamonds. She cannot bring forth new life in the sweat and agony of gestation.

The octet of the sonnet presents woman as sea; the sestet presents the woman as a star. The star is one of cold mineral light. As the sea, as perfect harmony in serene movement, she is indifferent to earthly travail. *Elle se développe*: within herself, within the constant rearrangement of the patterns which display her elements, within the progression of all that harmony which she drives before her like a network of sea-billows—*comme les longs réseaux de la houle des mers*—there is endless fascination and tranced contemplation. When her marine movement has been established, we are shown the texture of her reflecting surfaces—the desert sands, the azure, the metals in which she encloses herself so that she can be a mirror of cold light.

Her ritual of stately movement, her chant expressed in an effortless imperceptible dance, is the *volupté* of harmony and correspondence, of reciprocal fitness in all the relations which fuse together to form a swaying, floating, flowing cosmos whose effigy is woman and sea, mystically united. The sea, the ship, and the woman are a representation of the entranced state of the soul when all corresponds, when all the landscapes shape and melt into symbols, when the mind has drawn external reality into its own pattern, reforming it ideally. The poet's personality subsumes the external world, which develops as his personal manifestation: "What a great delight is that of drowning one's sight in the immensity of the sky and of the sea! . . . All these things think through me, or I think through them (for in the grandeur of reverie, the ego loses itself quickly!). They think, I say, but musically and picturesquely, without quibbles, without syllogisms, without deductions."

This idealistic epistemology is close to pantheism. But Baudelaire does not glorify nature as a God which absorbs man. He finds in *volupté* and correspondence a means of knowing—an epistemology, but not an eschatology of the ultimate religious truths. Baudelaire, the city-poet of emotive states, finds interest in no part of the countryside, but in the ship and the sea he sees a projection of himself.

Even sorrow provides *volupté*—"sorrow expressed rhythmically and cadenced fills the spirit with a calm joy," as in "Recueillement":

Sois sage, ô ma Douleur, et tiens-toi plus tranquille.
Tu réclamais le Soir; il descend; le voici . . .

Ma Douleur, donne-moi la main; viens par ici,

Loin d'eux. Vois se pencher les défuntes Années,
Sur les balcons du ciel, en robes surannées;
Surgir du fond des eaux le Regret souriant;

Le Soleil moribond s'endormir sous une arche,
Et, comme un long linceul traînant à l'Orient,
Entends, ma chère, entends la douce Nuit qui marche.

Be wise, O my Sorrow, and hold yourself more quietly.
You asked for Evening; he descends; here he is . . .

My Sorrow, give me your hand; come this way,

Far from men. See the deceased Years leaning
Over the balconies of the sky in old-fashioned gowns;
Smiling Regret springing up from the depth of the waters;

The moribund Sun going to sleep under an arch,
And, like a long shroud dragging from the East,
Listen, my dear one, listen to the soft Night which walks.

In the world of harmony, where there is no solid ground, one walks through vaporous textures of varying density. In this soft cosmos, sorrow can be a loved girl led by the hand and shown the mammoth nebulous scenery of the sunset. It is as if this scenery contained a number of huge, barely floating clouds and Sorrow were a child that pushed them softly, bounced them up a little, and let them settle in a slightly different pattern. The Years, Regret, the Sun, and the Night are resilient and easy for Sorrow to displace, like gigantic sponges. Regret is a smiling porpoise, bouncing from the tenuous watery depths. Having been laid away in the Past to sleep, the Years are gowned in drowsiness and tenuousness. They can be seen only at sunset when the texture of the air is soft and the colors are mild pastels, feathery without brilliance. The balconies appear only at sunset when the clouds are colored for the purpose. Then the Years awaken in their gowns of sleep, lean over the parapet and watch the light drain away from the scene. The fat sun, very round and paralyzed with drowsiness, is dropping without resistance and closing his eye under an arch of clouds;

and Night walks subtly over the scene, sweeping her shrouding skirts over the dreamers. She makes no noise in thus sweeping her train. Yet the darkness swelling up high to the zenith from the East can be heard by all the senses in unison, dazed in *volupté* as they are:

Entends, ma chère, entends la douce nuit qui marche.

Listen, my dear one, listen to the soft night which walks.

The scene is a trance in which Sorrow, enchanted, is a soft thrill in the blood, an indolent warmth in the depths of an attention which is fixed on *luxe, calme, et volupté*. Thus harmony and correspondence of the senses with the scene can transmute sorrow into serene dreaming and fascination of slow rocking and effortless movement around an ineffable still point:

Entends, ma chère, entends la douce nuit qui marche.

This *volupté* of harmony and trance is the sensual experience of the satisfaction of ". . . that immortal instinct of the beautiful which makes us consider the earth and its spectacles as an insight, as a correspondence of the heavens. The insatiable thirst for all which is beyond and which reveals life is the most living proof of our immortality.

"It is both by poetry and across poetry that the soul catches a glimpse of the splendors situated behind the tomb."

Baudelaire's celebrated "Le Balcon" presents earth and flesh as an insight into the other world of the spirit. The poem deals with incarnation. The flesh discloses the spirit; the spirit extends itself into the flesh. The flesh is luminous and spiritualized, as if it were an airy, palpable spirit. The earth and the flesh dissolve into forms of soft radiant light and active shadow, as if the forms were filled with fireflies or with luminous slowly moving molecules which spiraled into soft collisions. The celestial body of the woman acts as a link between the two worlds. Through worship of this ideal woman, this Beatrice, the poet, like Dante, seeks communion with paradise, the world of eternal forms.

T. S. Eliot has said that the adoration in this poem is of "something which cannot be had *in* but which may partly be had *through* personal relations." It is an apprehension of beatitude through fleshly love. Paul Valéry mentions the *sensualité puissante et abstraite* of the poem. The flesh is a vaporous enticing texture shaped into a symbol, an incarnation of one of the eternal forms:

> Rien ne vaut la douceur de son autorité;
> Sa chair spirituelle a le parfum des Anges,
> Et son œil nous revêt d'un habit de clarté.

> Nothing can equal the gentleness of her authority;
> Her spiritual flesh has the perfume of the Angels,
> And her eye invests us with a garment of clarity.

The flesh of the woman is *chair spirituelle*, a mortal substance redeemed and charged with transcendence, linking the two worlds of flesh and spirit:

LE BALCON

Mère des souvenirs, maîtresse des maîtresses,
O toi, tous mes plaisirs, ô toi, tous mes devoirs!
Tu te rappelleras la beauté des caresses,
La douceur du foyer et le charme des soirs,
Mère des souvenirs, maîtresse des maîtresses!

Les soirs illuminés par l'ardeur du charbon,
Et le soirs au balcon, voilés de vapeurs roses,
Que ton sein m'était doux! que ton cœur m'était bon!
Nous avons dit souvent d'impérissables choses
Les soirs illuminés par l'ardeur du charbon.

Que les soleils sont beaux dans les chaudes soirées!
Que l'espace est profond! que le cœur est puissant!

En me penchant vers toi, reine des adorées,
Je croyais respirer le parfum de ton sang.
Que les soleils sont beaux dans les chaudes soirées!

La nuit s'épaississait ainsi qu'une cloison,
Et mes yeux dans le noir devinaient tes prunelles,
Et je buvais ton souffle, ô douceur, ô poison!
Et tes pieds s'endormaient dans mes mains fraternelles!
La nuit s'épaississait ainsi qu'une cloison.

Je sais l'art d'évoquer les minutes heureuses,
Et revis mon passé blotti dans tes genoux.
Car à quoi bon chercher tes beautés langoureuses
Ailleurs qu'en ton cher corps et qu'en ton cœur si doux?
Je sais l'art d'évoquer les minutes heureuses!

Ces serments, ces parfums, ces baisers infinis,
Renaîtront-ils d'un gouffre interdit à nos sondes,
Comme montent au ciel les soleils rajeunis
Après s'être lavés au fond des mers profondes?
—O serments! ô parfums! ô baisers infinis!

THE BALCONY

Mother of memories, mistress of mistresses,
O you, all my pleasures! O you, all my duties!
You will remember the beauty of the caresses,
The gentle sweetness of the hearth and the charm of the
    evenings,
Mother of memories, mistress of mistresses!

On evenings illuminated by the ardor of coal,
And evenings on the balcony, veiled with rosy vapors;
How soft to me was your bosom! How good to me was
    your heart!
We often said imperishable things
On evenings illuminated by the ardor of coal.

How beautiful the suns are in the warm evenings!
How profound is space! How puissant is the heart!

Leaning towards you, queen of those adored,
I believed I breathed the perfume of your blood.
How beautiful the suns are in the warm evenings!

The night thickened like a partition,
And my eyes in the darkness divined the very pupils of
    your eyes.
And I drank your breath, O sweetness, O poison!
And your feet fell asleep in my fraternal hands!
The night thickened like a partition.

I know the art of evoking the happy minutes,
And I revive my past crouched within your knees.
For what is the use of seeking your languorous beauties
Elsewhere than in your dear body and in your heart so
    gentle?
I know the art of evoking the happy minutes.

These oaths, these perfumes, these infinite kisses,
Will they spring up again from a gulf prohibited to our
    soundings,
Like the rejuvenated suns mount into the sky
After having washed themselves in the bottom of pro-
    found seas?
—O oaths! O perfumes! O infinite kisses!

The profound and harmonious sensuality of the poem—*sensualité puissante et abstraite*—flows quietly, irresistibly, and simply. The sensuality of the poem is a process by which the flesh is refined into cold flame. The process purges of mortality the raw materials offered to it and incandesces the spiritualized flesh. The flesh, transfigured, becomes pure symbol.

This sensuality which refines is a radiance produced by many images of warmth. The warmth is tempered so that it never is oppressive or hot. To it is added a restraint which might be called coolness, so that the opposed relative degrees of sensation are combined in a transcendence of the flesh through sensual knowledge. By displaying the flesh as simultaneously warm and cool, we reach beyond it. The warmth of *plaisirs*—pleasures—is offset by *devoirs*—duties; "mother of memories, mistress of mistresses" establishes a figure of tranquillity and ease. The *foyer*, the hearth, is juxtaposed with evening, which tempers its heat and purifies its radiance. The warm coal expresses its *ardeur* in relation to the dark of evening. The warmth of the caresses is cooled by the use of *la beauté* in relation to them. The serenity of the balcony in the *vapeurs roses* of sunset, tempers the warmth of the sweet bosom (*sein m'était doux*) and heart (*cœur m'était bon*).

The vastness of space—*que l'espace est profond!*—makes most apparent the power of the heart—*que le cœur est puissant!* The heart, compassing in its warmth the expanse of space, is once again equivalent to the sun in its radiance. The warmth of the sun is subdued, for it is seen at sunset: *Que les soleils sont beaux dans les chaudes soirées!* It is cool warmth, like the tempered serenity of the *puissant* heart, for the sun is about to be rejuvenated by being washed in the sea after it falls under the horizon—*lavé au fond des mers profondes.* The sensuality of the woman enters richly with *Je croyais respirer le parfum de ton sang*—I believed I breathed the perfume of your blood. The warm weight and current of the woman's blood requires sensual attention. But this sensuality is cool, like the heart which is radiant and tranquil, and like the expiring sun, which is washed and thus renewed in the cool sea.

In speaking of such a woman as this of "Le Balcon," Baudelaire remarked: "I would compare her to a black sun, if one could conceive of a black star pouring out light and happiness." The paradoxical black light is a light without much heat, a harmonious light which establishes correspondence and serenity. This dark light, like the cool heat, is a quality of the sensuality of the poem. The flesh displays its ultimate beauties and dazzles the senses. This display, and this dosage of the senses, arrange the flesh and the landscape so that they capture a form of the spirit. The flesh becomes an extension of a mysterious realm behind it: "Nature is an allegory, a mould, a design formed by the impression of a pattern."

Sensuality is linked with *douceur*, which is in part "the need for forgetting the ego in *chair extérieure*—exterior flesh." The *douceur* of the flesh appears in *le parfum de ton sang*—the perfume of your blood. The night thickens as the sensuality of the poem becomes more marked; it seems to enclose the pair in complete privacy like a partition. He drinks her breath, which is *douceur* of harmony and correspondence, but poison in the sense that it leads him to lose his ego in this harmony of *chair extérieure*.

The cool radiance of the heart and the drowning sun, the balcony, the ardent coal, the mother of memories—all act to transmute sensuality into an avenue for the incarnation of the spirit. The sensuality arranges the dancing of the senses so that as the choreography shifts they can achieve a pattern which is both in time and outside of time, linking the two realms.

Part of the success of the poem in making the flesh luminous and transcendent comes from the candid acceptance of the flesh. The feet, the knees, the breath, the bosom are simple physical details. Placed beside suns, balconies, hearts, thick night, and profound space, they take on a heavier burden of significance, yet retain their outline of physical form.

The most important element of the success of the poem is its rhythm. Many of the lines are exactly balanced in two complementary phrases. Each line of the poem is a unit rhythmically and, when viewed alone, has a meaning which is semi-independent of its surrounding lines. The lines are rounded so smoothly that they adhere to each other by friction, without the necessity of locks, hooks, and clamps. The pieces cling together as if magnetized, without any clumsy binding. They could have been settled in a number of sequences; it would seem that they found themselves, gravitating together naturally, and once joined, they fused permanently. When they fused, they formed a new integer which cannot be dissected without loss of the all-important internal relations which make the poem. The poem is a whole vastly greater than the sum of its component lines.

The imperial leisure of the rhythm is due somewhat to the plenitude of imagery and sufficiency of the lines. The individual lines do not urge the reader to drop readily to their successors in order to follow a dramatic development. They invite individual contemplation, like large gems in a casket, and one passes slowly and reluctantly from one stone to another. Each stanza has an enclosing line which is its beginning and end. These lines—

Mère des souvenirs, maîtresse des maîtresses . . .

Les soirs illuminés par l'ardeur du charbon . . .

Que les soleils sont beaux dans les chaudes soirées . . .

La nuit s'épaississait ainsi qu'une cloison . . .

are of inexhaustible interest and implore reconsideration. Their repetition contributes to the serenity and stately movement of the poem. We are jealous of leaving them; we move through the poem more slowly and become more subject to its rhythm and suggestion. In addition, the repetition of these lines rounds out each stanza by enclosure so that each stanza is a unit, in itself inviting repeated attention. The lines are units; the stanzas are greater units; the poem is the greatest. The units fit so closely, as I have said before, that no cracks are visible; the whole is magnetized together, and each unit gains exceedingly in suggestiveness by being assumed into the greater unit.

The development of the poem is without drama; it is purely contemplative, but contemplation is effected through the senses alone. It is digestion of the treasure hauled in by the sensual nets. No ideas are contemplated; no philosophical observations or hints are made. But the result of this submission to the senses is an experience of harmony and correspondence. Through this sensual contemplation, as through Proust's timeless moments sensually discovered, that world of spirit and form is approached which could not be attained by philosophical meditation.

These remarks on the semi-independence of the lines and stanzas, the repetition of certain lines, the slow movement and slow rhythm, and the achievement of *sensual contemplation* in "Le Balcon" apply as well to its companion-piece, "Harmonie du Soir." In this remarkable poem, the natural landscape is made marvelously lustrous and sonorous, a fabulous artifice, a work of art like *le lustre*, the chandelier which Baudelaire describes elsewhere:

"What I have always found most beautiful in a theater is the chandelier, a beautiful object, luminous, crystalline, complicated, circular, and symmetrical.

"After all, the chandelier always appeared to me to be the principal actor seen through the big end or the little end of the opera glass."

In the poem, the harmony extends beyond the visual and claims the senses of smell and hearing. The heart also is brought in, charging the luminous scene with sympathy and extending the sensual harmony to include that of emotive feeling.

HARMONIE DU SOIR

Voici venir les temps où vibrant sur sa tige
Chaque fleur s'évapore ainsi qu'un encensoir;
Les sons et les parfums tournent dans l'air du soir,
Valse mélancolique et langoureux vertige!

Chaque fleur s'évapore ainsi qu'un encensoir;
Le violon frémit comme un cœur qu'on afflige;
Valse mélancolique et langoureux vertige!
Le ciel est triste et beau comme un grand reposoir.

Le violon frémit comme un cœur qu'on afflige,
Un cœur tendre, qui hait le néant vaste et noir!
Le ciel est triste et beau comme un grand reposoir;
Le soleil s'est noyé dans son sang qui se fige . . .

Un cœur tendre, qui hait le néant vaste et noir,
Du passé lumineux recueille tout vestige!
Le soleil s'est noyé dans son sang qui se fige . . .
Ton souvenir en moi luit comme un ostensoir!

HARMONY OF THE EVENING

Here are come the times when vibrating on its stem
Each flower evaporates as if it were a censer;
The sounds and the perfumes turn in the evening air,
Melancholy waltz and languorous vertigo!

Each flower evaporates as if it were a censer;
The violin trembles like a heart that is being afflicted;
Melancholy waltz and languorous vertigo!
The sky is sad and beautiful, like a great open-air altar.

The violin trembles like a heart that is being afflicted;
A tender heart, which hates the vast black nothingness!
The sky is sad and beautiful like a great open-air altar.
The sun has drowned in his blood which is congealing . . .

A tender heart, which hates the vast black nothingness,
Gathers every vestige of the luminous past!
The sun has drowned in his blood which is congealing . . .
Your memory in me gleams like a monstrance!

The poem is composed of ten lines in which the poet, who "is sovereignly intelligent, who is intelligence par excellence," renders "l'analogie universelle, or what a mystic religion calls correspondence." Each of these ten lines is a *lustre*, a beautiful object, luminous, crystalline, complicated, circular, and symmetrical, like the *valse mélancholique*, the censer, the turning air, the heart, the altar, the drowned sun, the luminous past, and the gleaming monstrance.

Each line deserves to be taken down from the shelf, to be contemplated in sunlight, firelight, and lamplight, and then returned to its place. Each line reverberates and corresponds with the rest to set up by sympathetic vibration the greater poem which is their harmony. The lines are arranged and rearranged so that they may interact with different pairs of lines and create fresh harmonies from new relationships. The fecundity of the language is illustrated by the subtle alterations of coloring given to the lines when they are repeated in different combinations. Thus the line

Valse mélancolique et langoureux vertige

has a quality of ecstasy and dream when associated with flowers and *Les sons et les parfums tournent dans l'air du soir*. But when placed between the afflicted heart of the violin and the sad altar sky, its quality is that of sympathy and drowsy pleasurable sorrow. Likewise, in

Un cœur tendre qui hait le néant vaste et noir!

A tender heart, which hates the vast black nothingness!

the heart is defeated by *le néant* in stanza three, where it is surrounded by the afflicted heart of the violin, the sad altar-sky, and the drowned sun. But in the fourth stanza, the heart conquers *le néant* and carries the drowned sun with it to victory by defeating time and space through memory—memory of the entire luminous past and dazzling redeeming memory of his saving queen, his Beatrice.

As the poem begins

Voice venir les temps où vibrant sur sa tige
Chaque fleur s'évapore ainsi qu'un encensoir,

Here are come the times when vibrating on its stem
Each flower evaporates as if it were a censer,

we note that *les temps* is in the plural; there is no one "time" of sunset; there is a numberless succession of times and degrees and nuances in the sun's glorious *coucher*. At sunset, the flowers expand their perfumes and vibrate on their stems, giving themselves harmonious motion as well as odor and form. The vibration of the flowers supports their comparison to a swinging censer evaporating its scent. Censer and flower are both circular and porous, exhaling their fragrance as they shake.

> *Les sons et les parfums tournent dans l'air du soir.*

> *The sounds and the perfumes turn in the evening air.*

The sounds, aside from the numerous ones implied but unmentioned, are those of the violin. The perfumes, among others, are those of the vibrating flowers. The sounds and the perfumes strike up harmonies; they commingle and undulate, striking both senses at once as if they were a single sensation. Their movement as they *tournent dans l'air du soir* is

> *Valse mélancolique et langoureux vertige!*

> *Melancholy waltz and languorous vertigo!*

The vibration of the flowers on their stems is part of the waltz. The vertigo, or dizziness, is due to the overwhelming of the senses by such sights, sounds, and odors. The slow turning of *les sons et les parfums* and the swaying of the flowers makes it a stately waltz of slow movement. The music for the waltz is provided by

> *Le violin frémit comme un cœur qu'on afflige,*

> *The violin trembles like a heart that is being afflicted,*

but before the music is provided, the line in which the flower evaporates like a censer is repeated at the beginning of the second stanza, to confound the two sensations and thus enhance the harmony.

There are three living things in the poem: the flower, the violin, and the heart. The sun is alive also, because in this poem it once again represents the heart. This heart is the heart of sympathy and suffering; it is afflicted; it trembles—

Un cœur tendre qui hait le néant vaste et noir!

A tender heart, which hates the vast black nothingness!

The heart adds emotive feeling to the sensual harmony and brings it to life by infusing the harmony with its emotion until they are composite. The living heart fears the blackness and void and seeks love. But like the puissant heart of "Le Balcon," it conquers profound space and time when it

Du passé lumineux recueille tout vestige!

Gathers every vestige of the luminous past!

The past, a lustrous intricate work of art, like Baudelaire's chandelier, is in this poem a serene backward extension of the present. All time past and present is harmonious because only the veins of luminous ore have been salvaged from the past by the heart. The present moment is thus not isolated in its correspondence and rhythm. By connection with a luminous past, its harmony is a harmony of all time as well as a harmony so absolute that it removes the consciousness of time. The heart, in gathering and infolding the past in this present harmony, has made all time present and observable at the one instant. The heart is expanded spatially by its customary Baudelaire attribute. As the sun, it scatters itself over the immense sky:

Le soleil s'est noyé dans son sang qui se fige . . .

The sun has drowned in his blood which is congealing . . .

The sun has blood, just as the heart does. This fine image calls up a sea of blood in which the sun can vaguely be seen, sinking beneath the surface. When the sun sets, the flames he leaves behind gradually sink lower and lower, just as when blood congeals, it shrinks down to occupy less space, darkening its crimson likewise.

Le ciel est triste et beau comme un grand reposoir.

The sky is sad and beautiful like a great open-air altar.

Only at sunset or sunrise can the sky be an altar. The quietness, the softness of the light, and the canopy of color fit the evening sky to be a temporary field altar which is immense in the stillness. The spectacle of the sunset sky as an altar holds our long attention, and causes a stop, a still point in the poem. The stately movement is resumed in the slipping of the sun below the horizon.

But the final line stops the poem completely and holds the attention permanently, so that there is no challenge to transfer it to something else. This line shines perpetually in visible vibrations of light; there is no movement in it other than this, and no change. It utterly satisfies the attention; and brings the poem to rest:

Ton souvenir en moi luit comme un ostensoir!

Your memory in me gleams like a monstrance!

The monstrance gleams in the last rays of the setting sun (*son sang qui se fige*) which continue to strike it even after the sun is apparently below the horizon because the monstrance is elevated on high. The sky at sunset provides a vast open-air altar (*reposoir*) for the exhibition and elevation of this Host. The monstrance or ostensorium is an ecclesiastical vessel for the exhibition of the Host, made of polished gold and surrounded by rays and fins of the precious metal, so that it seems to be a rosy star pulsating into space when sunlight strikes it. The memory of his ideal queen takes the place of the Host. This memory, in the form of a monstrance, illuminates the sky after the sun has drowned, apparently taking the place of the sun as the origin of light and radiance. But actually, from its elevated point, it is reflecting the sun's light, although the sun has sunk too low to be observed by the worshiper. This reflection of light is rich in meaning: the sun is really the heart, and the memory of his queen gleams like a monstrance from the light emitted by his own heart of sun.

The sunsets of "Le Balcon" and "Harmonie du Soir," still the observer in sensual contemplation, so that he mediates through the senses and captures the supernatural through absolute harmony of the senses: "The supernatural —intensity, sonority, limpidity, vibrativity, profundity, and resonant reverberation in space and in time."

10

After prolonged surrender to harmony and universal rhythm, ennui sets in. Even *volupté* is a prey to this "most hideous animal in the infamous menagerie of our vices." "It is a great delight to drown one's sight in the immensity of the sky and the sea! . . . Nevertheless, these thoughts, whether they proceed from me or rush from things themselves, soon become too intense. Energy in *volupté* creates an uneasiness and a positive suffering. . . . And now the profundity of the sky dismays me; its limpidity exasperates me. The insensibility of the sea, the immutability of the spectacle, revolt me."

When *volupté* is dissipated, the will remains relaxed. The universe has lost its savor; there is nothing of interest, only colorless masses. The poem for this is "Le Goût du Néant." The state of mind is not dreadful, but casual, acrimonious, and weary. Spiritual preoccupations become a joke. And the leaden "taste for nothingness" and extinction underlines the difficult smiles in the poem. There is a smile even in the final avalanche. Fascination with nothingness keeps the will relaxed. There is no sin, no good or evil, in this isolation. The victim, casual, acrimonious, and weary, is utterly lost. "How absurd!" he says, "I am lost!" Ennui is possibly the exquisite form of anguish. It brings complete isolation, for one's troubles are stale troubles and both worlds are unreal. The victim, as in Dante, is cut off from this world and from the next. The ego has no perceptions to divert it.

LE GOÛT DU NÉANT

Morne esprit, autrefois amoureux de la lutte,
L'Espoir, dont l'éperon attisait ton ardeur,

Ne veut plus t'enfourcher! Couche-toi sans pudeur,
Vieux cheval dont le pied à chaque obstacle butte.

Résigne-toi, mon cœur; dors ton sommeil de brute.

Esprit vaincu, fourbu! Pour toi, vieux maraudeur,
L'amour n'a plus de goût, non plus que la dispute;
Adieu donc, chants du cuivre et soupirs de la flûte!
Plaisirs, ne tentez plus un cœur sombre et boudeur!

Le Printemps adorable a perdu son odeur!

Et le Temps m'engloutit minute par minute,
Comme la neige immense un corps pris de roideur;
Je contemple d'en haut le globe en sa rondeur,
Et je n'y cherche plus l'abri d'une cahute!

Avalanche, veux-tu m'emporter dans ta chute?

TASTE FOR NOTHINGNESS

Gloomy spirit, formerly enamoured of struggle,
Hope, whose spur used to stir your ardor,
No longer wants to sit astride you! Lie down without
    shame,
Old horse whose foot stumbles on every obstacle.

Heart, be resigned; sleep the sleep of the brute.

Conquered, foundered spirit! For you, old marauder,
No longer does love have savor, no more than disputation;
Adieu then, songs of brass and sighs of the flute!
Pleasures, tempt no longer a somber sullen heart!

The lovable springtime has lost its odor!

And Time swallows me minute by minute,
As the immense snow swallows a body frozen stiff;
I contemplate from above the globe in its roundness,
And look no longer for the shelter of a hovel!

Avalanche, will you sweep me away in your downfall?

Taste for nothingness, "Le Goût du Néant," is a loss of will, a loss of hope. It is different from despair; it is blank and tasteless. *L'Espoir, dont l'éperon attisait ton ardeur, ne veut plus t'enfourcher*—Hope, whose spur used to stir our ardor, no longer *sits astride us*, whipping us on, taunting us with a vision of peace and salvation. Despair exists when we have a vision of what we have lost. Thus despair is excruciating; it taunts and torments. But the desire for nothingness dissipates the vision.

> *Couche-toi sans pudeur,*
> *Vieux cheval dont le pied à chaque obstacle butte.*

> Lie down without shame,
> Old horse whose foot stumbles on every obstacle.

It is a taste for the torpor of the brute animal. The drama of sin and salvation, despair and hope, becomes a dumb-show, a pantomime seen from an immense dream distance, meaningless.

> *Avalanche, veux-tu m'emporter dans ta chute?*

> Avalanche, will you sweep me away in your downfall?

If damnation and separation from the love which moves the universe arouse only a dumb stare, why not let the whole thing slip past, like a cascade of gigantic snowballs? "Le Goût du Néant" indicates the dangers of *volupté*. When the senses have been subject to the rhythm of sunset spaces and seascapes, exasperation with those same colors, forms, and movements leaves no interest to compensate for their loss. The contemplator has become drenched in a colorless, static world of fog.

Hope, the savage horseman, has dismounted, leaving us likewise without interest, without desire for the struggle. Therefore, unconsciousness is desired. Love, dispute, pleasures, springtime, are tasteless to the old marauder—*vieux maraudeur*—who had preyed on them all for sustenance.

Maraudeur is a playful appellation; the marauder is one who has stalked among his sensuous sustenance as one would walk among a maze of flowerbeds. His excursions were supported by *chants du cuivre*—songs of brass. This striking phrase is the phrase of pure brass and musical copper. The sweetness of hautboys, the round purity of the flute, the volume of the trumpet, are combined in one metallic, blooming horn. The *vieux maraudeur*, in his time of jubilance, had once had this tone carried close behind his trembling ears. The *vieux cheval*—old horse—a playful, homely term for a man in such distress, survives all this expense of exhilaration; exhilaration which is summed up in *chants du cuivre*. The heart (*cœur*) must resign itself to the loss of its vision of peace and be relieved of anguish, having given up the struggle.

Résigne-toi, mon cœur, dors ton sommeil de brute.

Heart, be resigned, sleep the sleep of the brute.

And so the insensible man is drifted over with the snow of time, time of which he now has no consciousness.

Et le Temps m'engloutit minute par minute,
Comme la neige immense un corps pris de roideur.

And Time swallowed me minute by minute
Like the immense snow swallows a body frozen stiff.

For one neither exhausts the time nor conquers time as in *volupté*, nor waits impatiently for it to pass as in *ennui*. It builds up around us and extinguishes us, without perceptible duration to the process. And if we no longer comprehend any familiar time, we are swallowed up into it. Which means we are falling asleep. We had previously been balanced only perilously upon the shelf of consciousness, consciousness which we measure by our comprehension of time. Not knowing time is the sign that we have tumbled off the shelf. *Résigne-toi, Couche-toi, Adieu donc*—the poem has the tone of preparation: Lay you down to sleep, *esprit vain-*

cu, *fourbu*. The concluding avalanche would be melodramatic and out of key were it not for the fact that we have been prepared for sleep. So the avalanche is without noise and is seen whimsically from an infinite distance:

Je contemple d'en haut le globe en sa rondeur.

I contemplate from above the globe in its roundness.

The poem falls out gracefully:

Avalanche, veux-tu m'emporter dans ta chute?

Avalanche, will you sweep me away in your downfall?

The most violent natural phenomenon is no more than a whisper after the preparation of the previous stanzas.

The avalanche is nevertheless merely a wish; it cannot choke up *le gouffre*: the gulf, the abyss. Insensibility is not possible. *Volupté*, the loss of taste for *volupté*, the consequent loss of desire ("Le Goût du Néant") and the long phase of excruciation and despair, form a repeating cycle. Over the cycle, insensibility hovers as an escape ladder. In the long phase of the cycle, Baudelaire is made of an electric framework of desires and egotism. He upholsters this frame with black velvet padding and tries to live within it. And again, he tries *volupté*; he tries unconsciousness. But his padding is flimsy and the wires, incandescing with the fury of desire, burn through it. Baudelaire is then left to live within this intricacy of red-hot filaments. He even finds them impressed on the visible surfaces which he grasps.

This is by way of saying what the abyss was for Baudelaire. Pascal carried the abyss with him; but Pascal's black velvet padding was thick and durable. He knew it was possible for him to slide down the gulf into the most depraved fancies, desires, and actions. But that knowledge carried him further into prayer and devotion. Baudelaire's flimsy padding is at once consumed. His mind is a sea of fancies, of desire, and of egotism. So that what to Pascal is a ceaseless itch in his background substance, is for Baudelaire a tight ring of fire around the skull. Baudelaire is possessed by it; his mind swims with fancies: *cauchemar multiforme et sans trêve*—multiform and truceless nightmare.

The abyss is the state of subjection to these exhausting desires. Not that they are accepted; but that they cannot be shut out.

LE GOUFFRE

Pascal avait son gouffre, avec lui se mouvant.
—Hélas! tout est abîme,—action, désir, rêve,
Parole! et sur mon poil qui tout droit se relève
Mainte fois de la Peur je sens passer le vent.

En haut, en bas, partout, la profondeur, la grève,
Le silence, l'espace affreux et captivant. . . .
Sur le fond de mes nuits Dieu de son doigt savant
Dessine un cauchemar multiforme et sans trêve.

J'ai peur du sommeil comme on a peur d'un grand trou,
Tout plein de vague horreur, menant on ne sait où;
Je ne vois qu'infini par toutes les fenêtres,

Et mon esprit, toujours du vertige hanté,
Jalouse du néant l'insensibilité.
—Ah! ne jamais sortir des Nombres et des Êtres!

THE GULF

Pascal had his gulf, moving with him.
—Alas, all is abyss—action, desire, dream,
Speech! and on my hairs which stand up on end
Many times I feel the breath of Fear.

Up above, down below, everywhere, is depth, the place
  of execution,
Silence, frightful and captivating space. . . .
On the substance of my nights, God with his savant finger
Draws a multiform and truceless nightmare.

I fear sleep as one fears a great hole,
All full of vague horror, leading one knows not where;
I see only the infinite through all the windows,

And my spirit, always haunted by dizziness,
Envies the insensibility of nothingness.
—Ah! never to go out from Numbers and Beings.

Tout est abîme—action, désir, rêve, Parole!—all is abyss—
action, desire, dream, and speech. The subject stands on a
pinnacle surrounded by these alternative pits. Action is before him; it can immensely strengthen his cruel desire by
putting it into practice. This means his feverishness, throb-
bing of the temples, and anguish would be intensified.
Action requires a motive and an assent. One must judge
just what it is possible to release from the mind into the
sphere of action. One must foresuffer the consequences of
this release. One must unite the past with the present and
force the mind to cohere upon the point of action. This
requires scrutiny and intensity of focus; an exhausting expense of will and of laborious balance. The abyss is in the
choice of alternatives, or rather in the will, which would
rather have its holiday and beg the exercise. For the exercise ransacks all reserves of balance and leaves the subject
naked to the abyss. The will is relaxed in volupté; it attempts
to extinguish itself in the "taste for nothingness," and ex-
cruciatingly blooms in le gouffre. Willy-nilly, one must be
alive and bristling, subject to fear, hope, and dizziness.

True action requires excursion into the abyss; the will
on each occasion sums up the good and evil which resides
in the subject from the past, and then reaches its balance.
Thus the past must be examined minutely and rapidly. The
result of the examination is often terror at the residue of
evil: mainte fois de la Peur je sens passer le vent—many
times I feel the breath of Fear passing. Desire likewise is
abyss; desire exacts evil and suffering from the victim in
which it is rooted. And by désir Baudelaire means every

concupiscence, every ambition, every vanity and pride, not merely desires of the flesh. With the Apostle Paul, with St. Augustine and Pascal, Baudelaire marks desire as the abyss because it is slavery and loss of freedom.

Yet desire is part of the will's freedom. Le gouffre accompanies the gift of free will, the gift which establishes man as a responsible spirit. Man is free to desire and free to act; but he needs, far above these, freedom *from* desire. The responsibility of action requires man to summarize his life at each step; that is, to enter the abyss. The slavery to desire is the matter of which man must make summarization. In the mind, desires are proposed and contemplated in rapid succession. If they cannot be controlled, the gift of freedom becomes a nightmare.

> Sur le fond de mes nuits Dieu de son doigt savant
> Dessine un cauchemar multiforme et sans trêve.

> On the substance of my nights, God with his savant finger
> Draws a multiform and truceless nightmare.

Parole is likewise an abyss, which implies some sort of theory of symbolism. Multiple meanings lie beneath the surface of speech and are contained by suggestion in the formal skin of speech. Speech represents the abyss by hinting at the multiple evocations of every word. A phrase may communicate any one of a number of variations of meanings. In addition to its burden as symbol, speech must cross an abyss in order to set up communication between individuals. To make a sortie from his isolated pinnacle surrounded by alternatives, one must muster his scattered personality into communicable and respectable form. The sortie requires a search for presentable material and a suppression of corruption. So speech is an abyss; it has many meanings; it is a selection of the controversial subject matter of the spirit; it indicates as symbol that the slightest verbal expression is a link with the intimate passions; it is an attempt to put two isolated beings into communication. Dream is abyss; it is descent—*le rêve, le cauchemar.*

> *Pascal avait son gouffre, avec lui se mouvant.*
> *—Hélas! tout est abîme,—action, désir, rêve,*
> *Parole!*

> *Pascal had his gulf, moving with him.*
> *—Alas! all is abyss—action, desire, dream,*
> *Speech!*

Pascal's abyss followed him about hauntingly. But Baudelaire looks out and faces a precipice in every direction.

> *En haut, en bas, partout, la profondeur, la grève,*
> *Le silence, l'espace affreux et captivant.*

> *Up above, down below, everywhere, is depth, the place of*
>   *execution,*
> *Silence, frightful and captivating space.*

He cannot stir without falling over into suffering—into *action, désir, rêve, Parole.* His pinnacle is safe when he is under the spell of *volupté.* But when the cycle moves on and activates the will, dormant under *volupté,* he must step over the edge and writhe in the gulf of sinners, *la profondeur, la grève.* This is the place of execution. He cannot shut out his freedom and his desire. Consequently the will is tormented with alternatives. Consequently the sins of his past are reviewed.

> *J'ai peur de sommeil comme on a peur d'un grand trou.*

> *I fear sleep as one fears a great hole.*

Sleep is described as an abyss likewise, a great hole full of vague horror, aimless. In sleep nothing can be shut out. But especially in dreams the will has lost its balance. Every fancy is acted upon at once. The will cannot suppress a desire and prevent it from entering the sphere of action. A fancy has only to appear in order to become an action. In sleep, the actions are put out continuously and pile up in a tremendous entanglement. The victim is in a morass—*cauchemar multiforme et sans trêve*—multiform and truceless nightmare.

Je ne vois qu'infini par toutes les fenêtres.

I see only the infinite through all the windows.

He can see only himself. In introspection and isolation, he considers his own case. Outside there is only meaningless infinity, white and blurting. No need to go out there for help; there is nothing, nothing at all outside. Well, then, this little room has swallowed up the earth—*la profondeur, la grève, le silence, l'espace affreux et captivant* is all that remains. His fits of depression have given him an inkling of the release which unconsciousness could bring: *mon esprit, toujours du vertige hanté*—my spirit, always haunted by dizziness. The room with its silence and its torment of desire is for the moment the only conscious entity available. He envies the insensibility of all outside it:

Jalouse du néant l'insensibilité.
—Ah! ne jamais sortir des Nombres et des Etres.

Envies the insensibility of nothingness.
—Ah! never to go out from Numbers and Beings!

He cannot leave this windowed room. It is composed of particulars. Particulars are, of course, measured, formed, and ordered by number which, in the Platonic sense, regulates the universe. The conscious world is made up of numbers and of beings (creatures). Beyond number and being there is no consciousness. The final line of the poem gives us the concept of insensibility in Platonic terms by subtracting from the world (which is the room with windows) those two elements which make it sensible. When we go outside of (*sortir*) Number and Being, we go out through the windows of the little room. We go no-where. The poem, of course, states that this never can happen (*ne jamais sortir*). But the presence of infinity outside the windows is a goad and a constant reminder of the relief that insensibility could bring as an escape ladder from desire and from the exercise of will.

11

Un matin nous partons, le cerveau plein de flamme,
Le cœur gros de rancune et de désirs amers.[1]

We leave one morning, the brain full of flame,
The heart swollen with rancor and bitter desires.

THE VOYAGE BEGINS as a quest for a boundless pleasure, good,
or satisfaction which can exhaust every desire. The traveler
sets off with salt on his lips (the sel of St.-J. Perse). The salt
is a restless appetite for some inconceivable novelty, some
exotic land or seascape, or some vast woman which will,
when found, justify the profusion of human appetites and
indeed glorify their quest. Every exhilaration, every hint
intensifies the chase by sharpening this lust:

> . . . ils s'enivrent
> D'espace et de lumière et de cieux embrasés.

> . . . they are intoxicated
> With space and light and skies glowing like flame.

Most important, the young traveler is convinced that this
summum bonum actually exists. For a desire as vast as his
there must be a corresponding satisfaction:

> Pour l'enfant, amoureux de cartes et d'estampes,
> L'univers est égale à son vaste appétit.

> For the child, in love with maps and picture-prints,
> The universe is equal to his vast appetite.

[1] All these quotations are from "Le Voyage," the concluding poem
in Les Fleurs du Mal. Note the similarity between the lines here
quoted from "Le Voyage," especially the first two quotations, and
many sections in the Anabase of St.-J. Perse.

The universe is equal to his appetite, at first. But as the appetite devours whatever small scraps it comes upon, it grows immensely:

—*La jouissance ajoute au désir de la force.*
Désir, vieil arbre à qui le plaisir sert d'engrais,
Cependant que grossit et durcit ton écorce,
Tes branches veulent voir le soleil de plus près!

—*Enjoyment adds strength to desire.*
Desire, old tree for whom pleasure serves as manure,
While your bark increases and hardens,
Your branches wish to see the sun more closely!

Small enjoyments stimulate the growth of desire. It strives to approach the size of that limitless satisfaction which it hopes to find. The sun is the symbol here of this satisfaction. In default of transient pleasures, "imagination sets up its orgy": *L'Imagination dresse son orgie.* But desire has now outgrown all bounds. There is no object or entity in the natural cosmos which can quench it or even appease it. The search grows more feverish as it becomes known that no satisfaction can be found. The natural cosmos has been called upon to produce a supernatural good. But it is not equal to the vastness of the appetite. For what is sought in terms of material and sensuous satisfaction is actually the spiritual source of life and peace. The appetitive desire is a perversion of the zealous spiritual desire which seeks its communion with God in the supernatural or spiritual order. When perverted, this desire retains its zeal but ransacks the natural order for a pleasure, a satisfaction which is never accomplished. What Baudelaire requires is communion with the spiritual source. But he does not know it; he thinks he requires *satisfaction* or *pleasure,* which are by definition concerned with the natural order.

And pleasure, to a Baudelaire, can be complex and rarefied, as in the case of *volupté.* This is the dreamy release from desire and will; the surrender to harmony, rhythm, sunsets, smells, colors, sounds, tastes. It is a pagan exhilaration, very short-lived. But the existence of this ecstasy, even for short periods of time, leads one to believe that the boundless satisfaction which he seeks lies in the natural order and is akin to *volupté*. This is the taste of the pagan paradise of intricate, endless cadences and harmonious movements:

Venez vous enivrer de la douceur étrange
De cette après-midi qui n'a jamais de fin!

Come and intoxicate yourself with the strange sweetness
Of this afternoon which never has an ending!

This ecstasy, daze, and annulment of the senses should prolong itself infinitely, with endless choreography. But the afternoon ends quite suddenly and one finds: "Before him only a storm in which nothing new is contained, neither instruction nor sorrow."

The cosmos has been ransacked for novelty; there is nothing new, and of course nothing to learn. One cannot enflesh oneself or jeopardize oneself with love. Nor can ennui, when it occurs, allow any engagement with the roots and texture of life. Therefore there is no sorrow to bind one to his fellows. Neither will unconsciousness come, no matter how strong *le goût du néant*. One is left on the slender pinnacle which leads downwards in every direction into *l'abîme* —the abyss. The flickers and fancies of *volupté* do not compensate for the torments of desire.

But we have observed only one half of the situation. *Volupté* need not be exclusively pagan. It might signify joy in the Creation, the love of nature. It need not be the selfish siphoning of pleasure from the cosmos, the sunsets, the balanced ships, the harmonious sea waves. It does not necessarily lead to such immature and fulsome manifestos as this:

Plonger au fond du gouffre, Enfer ou Ciel, qu'importe?
Au fond de l'Inconnu pour trouver du nouveau!

> *To plunge to the bottom of the gulf, hell or heaven, what*
> *does it matter?*
> *To the bottom of the Unknown to find something new!*

The will's freedom will always be a burden because of the attractiveness of evil. But it need not be a disaster if subject to grace and the spirit. Desire is a perversion of love away from the supernatural order toward the natural order, the order which should have value only in relation to the Creator.

The Apostle Paul, St. Augustine, and Pascal tell us that desire seeks the gulf of nothingness. Baudelaire drafts the excursions of the spirit into this abyss. His religious significance lies in his actualization of the misery which desire brings to the spirit.

> —*Hélas! Tout est abîme,—action, désir, rêve,*
> *Parole!*

> —*Alas! All is abyss—action, desire, dream,*
> *Speech!*

In the state of desire, everything points downward to nothingness. Perched on your slender pinnacle, you are closed off from the spiritual order overhead. And so all roads— *action, désir, rêve, Parole*—lead to *le gouffre*. The abyss is in one sense the appetite for horror and filth, the putrefied nutriment of pleasure. But in another, it is Dante's abyss— being cut off from the Love of God. (We must beware of thinking of this as some kind of a physical impulse emanating from an Aristotelian Prime Mover.) If the heavens are sealed up, all roads lead downward.

We observe that Baudelaire has, among other things, described an Inferno. Infernos are easier to do than are Purgatorios and Paradisos because of the prodigious availability of material. But they are of equal religious significance.

How much of an allegory then are the poems? Baudelaire had an insight unusual for a man of the nineteenth century.

He discovered that he himself was in present danger of damnation and that his century likewise was damned, although for sins far worse than his. On both sides of the English Channel, one must return to the seventeenth century—to Racine, to Milton, to the Jacobean lyricists and late Elizabethan dramatists—in order to find men of letters who were conspicuously aware of the possibility of individual damnation. This was a difficult discovery for a man of the nineteenth century to make amid the press gang of nationalists, Darwinists, positivists, Transcendental Unitarians, industrial planners, communists, universal religionists, and prophets of science. We must remember that Baudelaire's century was the century of Auguste Comte, Charles Darwin, Whitman, Claude Bernard, Renan, Emerson, Hugo, George Sand, Zola, Taine, Herbert Spencer, and Karl Marx. Before, during, and after his lifetime, ideas and movements which Baudelaire regarded as accursed were dominant.

Baudelaire and Dostoyevsky confessed the existence of evil in human nature. The century was unsympathetic to their views. Did they not affirm the presence of the Devil? Not only the prose popularizers of biology and psychology, the Messieurs Homais, but also "advanced" theologians ridiculed the persistence of this concept. Indeed, it was as if the nineteenth century had banded together and agreed that one word "Devil" was taboo in polite society. If you spoke it out, you broke all the rules of the game, for the century was attempting, despite its apparent nonchalance, to prove more than anything else that evil did not exist in human nature. So that if you uttered the forbidden word, you betrayed your community and your century in its principal effort. But Nietzsche concluded the century by unconsciously attempting to incarnate a demon; which is to say that, in giving unbridled autonomy to the "will," he aroused that complete and organized egotism which is the satanic in human sin. Had all the precocity, the wit and brightness of the century's ideas been at its root merely hiding their eyes and pretending that the "Devil," that is, the satanic in human egotism, did not exist? But in that case there was little novelty. Jean-Jacques had cut the blooms before them, and long before him the fruit had been tasted in the Garden of Eden. The Tower of Babel had risen on a similar foundation. Nietzsche, by his very existence, unconsciously affirmed the failure of the century's precocious notions. In order to thrive, egotism requires that the ego be considered completely good. It denies that evil can exist within itself. But when egotism has been allowed its conditions under the license of the precocious ideas, it flourishes to such an extent that a Nietzsche is produced in the form of a devil. Out of the denial of the demonic, a demon is hatched. This denial of its demonic nature removes all curbs from the violent tumescence of egotism, which in its turn gestates an unmistakable demon of wickedness and pride. The new ideas were merely a blindness, an unwillingness to observe.

Baudelaire presented his century with allegory. He showed sin and the wages of sin. The despair and suffering he presents are spiritual afflictions brought about by the presence of evil in human nature; that is, by the demon within us. He is little concerned with the predominantly physical interests of his period.

We have examined poems which concern the attractiveness of evil, and poems which concern the suffering and remorse of the victim. These themes form *le gouffre*, *l'abîme*. Caution, prudence, moderation, are useless. The victim must be redeemed by saving grace. The poems are not posters for moral edification, saying "Profit by these examples." But they are allegorical in the sense that they actualize the sinner's helplessness when trapped in *le gouffre* of desire. *The allegorical sense is that there is such a thing as sin.* Hygiene and therapy may make every degradation sanitary and physically safe. But many people cannot live for very long as clean beasts. They cannot be brutalized sufficiently to annul the suffering of sin, peculiar to man alone. If the gulf, *le gouffre*, exists, sin exists and a man exists. His suffering is that, while lying at the bottom of the pit, he cannot remove his attention from the open mouth of the pit above him, through which he fell and by which he is shown his former purity. The sinner is primarily a fallen man, or even a fallen angel. There are other creatures at the bottom of the pit with him, as in

> *Un Ange, imprudent voyageur*
> *Qu' a tenté l'amour du difforme,*
> *Au fond d'un cauchemar énorme*
> *Se débattant comme un nageur, . . .*

> *Où veillent des monstres visqueux*
> *Dont les larges yeux de phosphore*
> *Font une nuit plus noire encore*
> *Et ne rendent visibles qu'eux.*

> *An Angel, imprudent traveler*
> *Whom love of the deformed has tempted,*
> *To the depths of an enormous nightmare,*
> *Struggling like a swimmer, . . .*

> *Where viscous monsters are watching*
> *Whose large phosphorescent eyes*
> *Make the night still blacker*
> *And make only themselves visible.*

But these creatures are beasts; they neither know nor care that they are at the bottom of the abyss. They swim contentedly in their element. Again the sinner's suffering can be qualified: it is the realization that he has taken the image of God which lies in himself and soiled it and mutilated it in emulation of the beasts who know no law but survival and desire. Baudelaire's poems show that sin is possible. The advanced thought of the century claimed it was impossible; the spirit, if it existed, could not be soiled.

Baudelaire's allegory is not overt. It possesses none of the usual trappings. He does not interrupt his work with abstract moralizations. By means of his command over language and metaphor and his selection of the exact sequence of material for his peculiar treatment, he makes actual (he does not merely state) certain spiritual predicaments in which the springs of action and desire are indicated. The experience which he has skillfully planned for us to have when we act in making the poem (by reading it), is, in many poems, one of the association of spiritual purity and the sense of beauty; of the opposite association of moral degradation and ugliness. As an example:

> Et nous alimentons nos aimables remords
> Comme les mendiants nourrissent leur vermine.

> And we feed our pleasant remorse
> As beggars nourish their vermin.

Self-satisfied remorse is pleasing; therefore we nourish and encourage it. But it is like vermin, we nourish it by giving it our blood to suck. We remember in "Au Lecteur" how the attractiveness of evil was presented in a series of metaphors linking it with repulsive objects or actions.

The connection between aesthetics and morality, as in "Femmes Damnées," is apparently a discovery by the reader, who thus participates in creating the poem. But of course it is laid there for him to stumble upon. This is the subtlest type of allegory; perhaps, strictly speaking, it is not allegory, but it is related. Baudelaire's experience fell into a pattern which marked sin as ugliness. This general pattern informs any Baudelaire poem. In turn, the poem orders and embellishes particular experiences so that another definite and single but related experience will be given to the reader. In this way Baudelaire's convictions enter his work. His allegory is like a huge organ pipe, vibrating too low for human ears, but nevertheless subtly pervasive.

Baudelaire shows; he does not state. And when we discover in his poems, seemingly by ourselves, some paradoxical truth (as in the examples given earlier in discussing "Au Lecteur," "L'Imprévu," "Femmes Damnées," and other poems), he is making an allegorical point; he is teaching us. When he has taught us that sin exists, the whole marvelous house is opened up; damnation and salvation appear on the horizon.

Not that Baudelaire was an ordered personality, propagating continuous wisdom. What he grasped, he had gained through distress. He was more of a touchstone than a sage. His "Voyage" (described earlier), his appetite for novelty and exotic lands and creatures, was at the beginning like the voyage of Flaubert's Madame Bovary. Somewhere the great satisfaction existed. They must find it, or else die of thirst. Emma Bovary made such extreme demands upon the cosmos for satisfaction that she fell in love with herself. Her ideal lover could not be found outside her own mind and was merely a projection of her personality. She was disgusted whenever she had her weekly rendezvous at Rouen with a flesh and blood lover, Léon, the lawyer's clerk. She dominated him and assumed him into her own personality. Her love letters, addressed in his name, were written to a splendid creature who existed only in her mind and who was really herself. The other six days of the week, she was less miserable. Sealed up in herself, she shuffled her own personality, reviewed it, split it in two and reunited it incessantly. But her shut-in-ness, her inability to make a sortie from the tower of her feverish personality consumed what little fuel she possessed for the feeding of such an exhausting flame. She burnt herself out in the sense that her ransacked personality in the end could no longer engage her interest. The world outside herself was dull and barren; she could no longer spread herself over it and subsume it under herself by painting it gaudy colors in her mind. Thus came her exasperation and suicide; the taste of ink, the noise of the mad beggar at her deathbed.

Baudelaire faced a similar exasperation. He found intermittent satisfaction for his thirst and desire in the momentary exhilarations of *volupté*. He did not find satisfaction solely within himself, as did Emma Bovary, but found it in a sense of temporary mystical union with nature. This is a bad thing if it is interpreted as a religious experience. But Baudelaire possessed the wisdom to assign it to its proper place as a joy in the Creation. The experience of *volupté* does not set up a Nature God. *Volupté* in addition extricates the personality from self-inspection and involves it with the external world. Unlike Emma Bovary, Baudelaire's suffering on account of desire led him to a consciousness of good and evil. The consciousness of sin is not the counsel of prudence: that some actions are physically or socially harmful. It is not reasoned whether an action or a thought is evil or not. It is ingrained as the incontestable will of God. The knowledge that some actions and desires are evil without there being any mere *reason* for their being evil is the first and most difficult step toward regeneration.

Though Bovary and Baudelaire start the voyage with the same ineluctable thirst of desire, the exhaustion of the cosmos by their desire leads them in different directions. Emma Bovary turns in upon herself and thrashes herself to bits. Baudelaire discovers the world of good and evil and is led out of himself to a relaticn with the Giver of Life through his consciousness of sin. Damnation and salvation rise above the distant horizon. He maintains his vision and his connection with a law and a Lord exterior to himself. He does not approach obedience or communion until the very end. But the knowledge that *he could do evil* gave him a confused awareness of God. Emma Bovary could not do evil because she had no knowledge of it. She knew only the expedient, the prudent, the pleasant, and their opposites. Baudelaire has made the arduous initial step toward regeneration. Bovary has no glimpse of regeneration. And it is a question of grace: to which shall the vision be granted and to which shall it be denied?

We are now prepared to evaluate Baudelaire's propagation of wisdom, his allegory. He has achieved the first step and displays the distress of the *conscious sinner*. His is not an ordered personality, but an excruciated one. Likewise his wisdom is wisdom of an inhabitant of Inferno, excruciated rather than ordered. The nearness of his distress is an advantage; the lack of order is a disadvantage. It is very difficult to have both. Dante preserved both order and the freshness of peril, suffering, and beatitude. Baudelaire provides us with the lenses of wisdom but fails to equip them with a focus. Each poem provides an example of wisdom, but they do not develop upon each other. There is no coherence of scheme, there are no ordered layers of thought building upward from the spectacle of sin.

The poems as facets reveal a disorderly central crystal. Baudelaire does not go beyond the initial step toward regeneration. His sensibility is chaotic. He cannot get beyond sin; sin is so immense it obscures the higher mansions. And so his wisdom is out of proportion. True, it has made the most difficult and most important step. But sin, although the most apparent of all, is merely one part of Christian doctrine. A disorderly Inferno which does not lead to higher realms is presented singly. By omission, the Christian wisdom is distorted, although that much of it which is presented is still valid.

The heresy which he approaches is Manicheanism, the assertion of the existence of an evil power equal and opposite to God. If this were the case, the sinner would be permanently lost, incapable of succor by Divine Grace. Damnation tends to eclipse salvation on Baudelaire's horizon. When one aspect of Christian doctrine is stressed at the expense of another, a heresy is produced. But at times Baudelaire descends to a Satanism which cannot be dignified as heresy. A rattling of skeletons and coffin lids, those *frissons* of terror which Hugo admired, can occasionally lay Baudelaire's convictions open to ridicule. But actually his Devil is not the Evil One of Edgar Allan Poe's tales of mystery. Nor is evil for him a Swinburnian parlor game to be played by dimming the lights and hanging the drawing room in black velvet.

The aesthetic of Poe and Baudelaire required short, well-made poems. In poems such as "La servante au grand cœur dont vous étiez jalouse," "Avec ses vêtements ondoyants et nacrés," "Je n'ai pas oublié, voisine de la ville," "Harmonie du Soir," "Le Goût du Néant," "Le Gouffre," "Spleen," "Chant d'Automne," "Le Balcon," and others, a rigorous and exquisite order is imposed upon the poet's selection of detail and sequence of ideas or impressions. These poems are concentrated in the extreme, with almost no loose fat. They cumulate rapidly, sternly, and simply, but without hastiness. Such precision and brilliance of metaphor compressed in so secure a space had not appeared since Andrew Marvell. The wild horse of the imagination works in a strong harness of order and form. Each presents its demands. As the demands are slowly resolved, a new entity, the poem, takes shape encouraged by their comparison and fusion. In the poem, imagination cannot be distinguished from form. Both are spontaneous and both unite to form an integer, a new element, not a compound formed of previous elements. This new element, the poem, is a discovery, clearly distinct from its preliminary operations. The preamble of horse and harness is merely a discipline required to induce the balance out of which a poem may grow.

Some of the larger poems, of which "Femmes Damnées" is the best example, are well sustained performances, but seem overgrown. One well-executed stanza succeeds another, but their development seems inconclusive. The poems have been allowed to ramble and ruminate. The result is dissipation of cumulative impact. Each stanza is in itself marshaled for attack. But the links between stanzas present not transitions to fresh developments and perspectives, but extensions and supplements. When a genuine modulation or movement is made, the effect is lost. The poem seems merely to ruminate within a succession of new channels which are in turn exhausted of complementary material. The individual stanzas are tightly composed and well stocked with brilliant metaphor. But they do not combine to form an organism. These larger poems are strings of fine pearls, connected by the mechanical agency of their silken strands. The nexuses are inconclusive; they are plus signs. They add on more treatment; but in the meantime the impetus of the poem has petered out. The impetus of a poem requires for its sustention shifts of tone, alterations of perspective, seizure of apparently disparate experience and demonstration of its congruence to the rest of the material of the poem. And this establishment of transitory nexus is incredibly difficult to perform. It is the principal problem of form.

For this reason, the shorter poems, as cited earlier, are Baudelaire's aesthetic and formal achievement. Certain larger poems, "Au Lecteur" and "La Béatrice," which are not so well made as the best shorter poems, possess considerable structural strength and good sustention of intensity of language and rhetorical impetus. There is subtlety in their use of nexus. Among the larger poems, "Femmes Damnées" is a well-sustained performance. But most of the longer important poems have in addition to the structural faults of "Femmes Damnées" a number of mediocre stanzas. Poems such as "A Celle Qui Est Trop Gaie," "L'Imprévu," "Les Petites Vieilles," "Une Voyage à Cythère," "Le Beau Navire," "L'Irrémédiable," "Le Voyage," and others, I have considered only in part. Each contains brilliant verses which make the poems memorable. And each contains dependable standard verses which fill in adequately, but are not distinguished. Perhaps Baudelaire was too lazy to drive the poems to their utmost possibility; perhaps he had reached in each one an impasse on his routes of development. Or again, he may have thought the poems were perfectly made as they stood.

Notwithstanding his failure to sustain a high level of intensity in most of his poems, it is apparent that Baudelaire was striving for the perfectly reduced poem, one of uniform high excellence, of which one verse could not be compared to the disadvantage of another. This was *ipso facto* the poem of perfect structure, because it was so skillfully joined that it could not be dismantled for the purpose of critical comparison of some of its components at the expense of others. The poorly constructed poems may be dismantled easily. Parts may be cut away from them and examined independently, without the loss of contextual support becoming a very great disadvantage.

The shorter poems cannot be sectioned. They are rigorously ordered. There are no seams, no crevices, no soft spots. Mr. R. P. Blackmur has remarked that Baudelaire, a disordered, excruciated man, expressed his disorder in a carefully ordered and disciplined poetic form. On the other hand, Whitman, whom I should like to consider as a complacent rather than an ordered man, expressed his complacency in a disordered poetic form. He congratulated himself and smugly celebrated his inexhaustible flux of sentiments, the value of which he could not doubt. Baudelaire's spiritual disorder is shown off at an advantage in his ordered rendering of his excruciation. Such a disordered state is actualized best in ordered form. We think of course of Dante and Racine, ordered personalities whose poetry is likewise ordered formally. *Inferno* and *Phèdre* portray and interpret spiritual disorder, but place it within its proper frame, and account for it. Baudelaire's disorder is not accounted for; it does not appear within the perspective of salvation, as with Dante and Racine. Baudelaire acquired this perspective personally as his life drew to its close. But his poems mainly concern sin and its ravages. We should not however expect too much of a frame and system of accounting from Baudelaire, inasmuch as his compressed lyric form is less comprehensive than that of Dante and Racine. In our own day, T. S. Eliot's religious poems have assumed a loose and rambling contemplative structure, to account for and frame the inter-relations of good and evil, or order and disorder; and the solutions and perspectives of salvation and damnation.

We must accord Baudelaire his seat within the poetic hierarchy. His skill in form and language broke him off from his predecessors, and made him the stem and starting point for subsequent French poetry and for English poetry from Pound and Yeats onward. Modern poetry learned from him the use of precise and compelling metaphor, the use of language both exactly clear and connotative, and the discriminating utilization of paradox, all of which had fallen into disuse since the seventeenth century. Baudelaire announces the decline of the era of vagueness, sentiment, and loose outpourings of personality. He upholds precision and clarity. He discloses precisely and clearly the nature of a given act or state of mind.

His language, in addition to this, produces subsurface relations of meaning which enhance the initial precision by délimiting more closely the quality of the act or state of mind described. To obtain this quality, precision is required first of all in the denotative, or apparent, surface meaning. This initial precision is refined by the addition of subsurface meanings which pare down the possibilities of meaning to the one or two which will satisfy all the conditions exacted by the metaphors. When this precision is applied, the hypocrisy which surrounds the principal dramatic situations found in the world falls away, and poetry of great power and passion may result. This precision is an intensity of focus which allows for maximum penetration by language of those surfaces of hypocrisy and euphemism which conceal the world of the conscience and which obstruct our attempt to use the natural world as a source for metaphors and symbols of spiritual states.

Baudelaire's excruciation likewise entitles him to a seat in the hierarchy, seeing that his disorder was expressed in an orderly form. His disorder presents a nakedness and lack of pretense which enables his skilled language to work up metal which is drawn directly from the furnace of lust, egotism, and the non-sensual desires. He was spiritually alive even in his degradation. He was never utterly lost because he knew that what he was involved in was evil.

Appearing at a time when debasing and brutish ideas were carrying all before them, he decried the Tower of Babel which had risen slowly on the foundations of the preceding two centuries and which was in Baudelaire's time beginning the rapid and patent construction of its superstructures. Now the idea of the time, of Comtists, Marxists, Fourierists, Darwinists, and of Freudians yet to come, was that man should live like a clean beast in material comfort, not subject to the anguish of conscience and spiritual distress. If all pleasures are made clean, easy, and available, there should be no occasion for a consciousness of sin. Man would then be freed from the cares of the body by material comforts and machine techniques; he would be freed from the cares of the soul by hygiene and psychoanalysis, whose mission was to dissipate the knowledge of sin and encourage the victim to be *healthy*. Of course, psychoanalysis belongs to the twentieth century, but it is a fulfillment of the trend. Healthy modern persons should not have obsessions such as sin. A spiritual life is a needless encumbrance in a world of efficiency and popular celebrations. A sanitary Tower of Babel inhabited by healthy animals was what the period offered to Baudelaire as an ideal.

Since, for all their hopes of attaining the blissful brutish state, men were not animals, being distinguished by insatiable egotism, they required a Tower of Babel to commemorate their egotism. Hygiene in low, flat, easily accessible buildings was not adequate. It was easy to make the people of the time forget that they were made in God's image. But men could not be rid of their cherished spirit of wickedness. So they failed in their attempt to become animals. Man's egotism erects the Tower, but since man is split into many languages and races, his egotism finally pulls it down, as we who inherit from him in this century can see. Behind the idea of Babel and hygienic brutishness is of course the nineteenth century's cardinal disavowal of the existence of evil in human nature.

Baudelaire, in his notebooks, *Fusées* and *Mon Cœur Mis A Nu*, marked the wickedness of his period as clearly as he marked George Sand as the contemporary temptress of its experiment with brutishness. He saw that man was being explained away as a purely physical and natural organism. In this way it was hoped that the dangerous and tormenting gift of freedom of will which set man off from the beasts could be gotten rid of. He would be determined by natural law, happy and careless. "Religious" sentiments could be satisfied by some form of naturalistic mysticism such as Whitman's or Hugo's. Baudelaire foresaw that freedom of will could not be suppressed; that it would erupt with egotism more and more savage the longer it was denied. We who stand among the ruins of this eruption which seems still to be approaching its climax cannot realize what an achievement it was for Baudelaire to have seized this wisdom at a time when the blind led the blind. Kierkegaard and Dostoyevsky had much less distance to travel than he.

Notre pauvre Baudelaire paid dearly for his final wisdom. His body and mind were exhausted by the long pilgrimage through despair, lust, and pride. He arrived in time to die. An imperfect man and an imperfect poet, he is the very type of the lost sinner saved and forgiven. He was reduced by his insatiable pride to humiliation wherein he grasped first damnation and ultimately salvation. We revere the skill and wisdom with which he actualized the life and distress of the spirit. We extend our sympathy to his acceptance of that humiliation which was necessary purgation and preparation for the inestimable grace of humility vouchsafed to him when he collapsed at Brussels. We commend his spirit into the hands of Our Lord who finally took upon Himself the burden which tortured this man.